D1480033

THE
ACCIDENTAL
SALES MANAGER

THE

ACCIDENTAL

SALES MANAGER

HOW TO TAKE CONTROL and LEAD YOUR SALES TEAM to RECORD PROFITS

CHRIS LYTLE

WILEY

JOHN WILEY & SONS, INC.

Published by John Wiley & Sons, Inc., Hoboken, New Jersey.
Published simultaneously in Canada.

For general information on our other products and services or for technical support, please contact our Customer Care Department within the United States at (800) 762-2974, outside the United States at (317) 572-3993 or fax (317) 572-4002.

Wiley also publishes its books in a variety of electronic formats. Some content that appears in print may not be available in electronic books. For more information about Wiley products, visit our web site at www.wiley.com.

Library of Congress Cataloging-in-Publication Data:

Lytle, Chris
    The accidental sales manager : how to take control and lead your sales team to record profits / Chris Lytle.
        p. cm.
    Includes Index.
    ISBN 978-0-470-94164-5 (cloth); ISBN 978-1-118-06391-0 (ebk);
ISBN 978-1-118-06392-7 (ebk); ISBN 978-1-118-06393-4 (ebk)
        1. Sales executives.   2. Sales force management.   3. Success in business.
    I. Title.
    HF5439.5.L98 2011
    658.8'102—dc22   2010053519

Printed in the United States of America

10 9 8 7 6 5 4 3 2 1

To Sarah McCann/Zola Gorgon
My two favorite characters in the world

CONTENTS

ACKNOWLEDGMENTS

For every sales manager, VP of sales, and CEO who agreed to talk to me for this book, I am forever grateful. Your stories and willingness to share your best practices make this a much better book than it would have been had I "gone it alone."

To everyone who has become a customer and a friend over the past three decades, I appreciate the trust you've shown in our products and programs. Whether you've purchased a book or audio product or flown me half way around the world to speak to your sales organization, it means a lot.

Thanks to Cliff Albert, Gary Buchanan, Tom Clevidence, Michael Draman, Phil Fisher, Ed Fratz, Ken Greenwood, Jay Leonardi, Jim Lobaito, Trey Morris, Dan Manella, Gary Miles, Tim McMahon, Sarah McCann, Garfield Ogilvie, Mark Peterson, Jeff Sleete, David Snodgrass, Kent Stevens, Richard Williams, Lowell Yoder, and Rod "Zeke" Zimmerman. I asked you a few questions, shut up and recorded your answers, transcribed them and all of a sudden half the book was written.

To the team at Wiley: I owe a big thank you to Dan Ambrosio for picking up the phone and asking me if I didn't want to write another book. Ashley Allison has been a patient and very fast editor, and Deborah Schindlar has kept the composition process going ahead of schedule despite my sometimes erratic writing patterns. Thanks for staying on top of things and challenging me to do the same.

ABOUT THE AUTHOR

Chris Lytle, the best-selling author of *The Accidental Salesperson*, had a lucrative but increasingly frustrating career as a professional speaker. He had an obsession with finding a better way to drive real behavior change.

He understood that adults learn by doing, not by hearing about how someone else did it. He was frustrated with the start-and-stop nature of training seminars and the limited results that an occasional learning event creates.

Unfortunately, that's what his customers thought they wanted.

Undeterred, he set out to reinvent the way he delivered his own training programs. Identifying his biggest competitor as the do-it-yourselfer, he decided to partner with sales managers who train their own people.

His website *Fuel* contains knowledge bites (digestible sales ideas) that can be consumed in five minutes or less and discussed for 25 more minutes in a meeting. Lytle coined the phrase "The Honors Class in Selling Instant Sales Meeting." Sales managers use his content to spark lively conversations about sales issues.

Along the way, he discovered how to add the missing ingredient—accountability—to the mix. Teaching managers how to add accountability to their training translated into immediate, bottom-line impact for tens of thousands of sales-people at every level of their careers.

Lytle is the president and product developer of Sparque, Inc. the Chicago-based company he runs with his partner/wife Sarah McCann. He still speaks on sales and sales management topics to a select group of clients. Increasingly, he delivers his content on his website and through short Webinars.

You may have had a gut feeling there is a better way to develop the people who develop your profits. Trust your gut.

You can get a free trial of Fuel by going to www.sparquefuel .com. Sales managers who want to see the full capabilities can request a "private tour" with Lytle. You can do that by e-mailing him at chris.lytle@sparque.biz or calling 1-800-255-9853.

INTRODUCTION

Congratulations on Your "Promotion"

I f you like to solve complicated puzzles, a career in sales management will keep you perpetually challenged. If you've just become a new sales manager, you're probably excited, a little nervous, and pretty curious about what to expect. Fortunately for you, this book will slash several years off of your learning curve. If, on the other hand, you've been at this sales management *thing* for a while, the information here will refocus and reenergize you.

This book will introduce you to some very successful sales managers who have made plenty of mistakes and chosen to share their experiences with you.

Being a sales manager in a time of continuous innovation and destabilizing change is challenging enough, and can even be quite overwhelming for many. But for those professionals who get their kicks from solving problems and furthering the skills and fostering the success of other people, sales management is a gratifying and rewarding job.

I don't know your story, but I clearly remember how—and when—I got my first sales management job. I was just 18 months into my current sales job, minding my own business and selling up a storm, when I got called into the general manager's office one day. Upon my arrival, two of the owners were sitting there.

"We're making you the sales manager," one of them said to me.

I was too young, startled, and flattered to refuse.

I had gotten into sales accidentally three years earlier. Now, I was being promoted. They weren't grooming me to move into management; as of the next Monday, I was *The Accidental Sales Manager*.

Don't worry; despite this fairly personal introduction, this is not an autobiography. Though I will share a variety of the sales management lessons I've encountered throughout my career—many of which I learned the hard way—my experiences and advice aren't the only ones you'll find here. To add depth and perspective, I have interviewed CEOs, VPs of sales, field sales managers, and one college professor. These successful leaders share know-how gained over many years of leading sales forces and meeting quotas. The conversations I've had with these remarkable people, who took the time to share both their joys and frustrations, reminded me of the tremendous responsibilities they agree to shoulder when they accept any kind of promotion. I made it a point to ask every single one of them two questions:

1. What do you wish you had known about sales management before you took on the job?
2. What did you have to learn about sales management the hard way?

You will benefit from their diverse perspectives. Selling is a shared experience that salespeople have all by themselves. Think about that. Your salespeople most likely believe that no one else is enduring the same price resistance, rejection, self-doubt, and fear of failure as they are. They don't realize that most other salespeople are calling on tough customers and having the same experiences all by themselves. Sure, they can discuss these issues over a drink with peers. But many salespeople today work a territory from their home office, and therefore have less interaction than ever with colleagues and people who can empathize with their situations. This feeling of isolation can become a significant problem. Getting a national sales team together for a quarterly sales meeting to share their experiences may be seen as an expensive luxury in today's economy. Indeed, increasingly sales meetings are done via conference call or Webinar. However you do it, getting salespeople to share their experiences and thereby inspire one another takes the pressure off you to train and motivate them. I offer you a pre-planned annual meeting in Chapter 6 that I have used with my clients to get the salespeople talking and make them the stars of the annual meeting.

Now let's get back to you and your job: Sales management is a shared experience you are having all by yourself—and that's exactly where this book comes into play. Your boss can promote you, but he's not always able to tell you how to become a successful sales manager. If you are part of a large company, you may be able to get some mentoring from a successful sales manager. But too many new sales managers find themselves on their own. And your track record of sales success, while admirable, will not translate into sales management success. Even if you were a veteran salesperson, you are a novice the second you become a sales manager. Maybe you've noticed this; I call it . . .

The Forgotten Rookie Syndrome

The new sales manager is almost always the forgotten rookie—forgotten because the person who promoted you considers you to be an experienced hand. And of course, you were an experienced hand—in sales. Now, however, you're an inexperienced sales manager.

Why does this forgotten rookie syndrome exist—and persist? Well, your boss has a tendency to promote you and then quit worrying about you. There's a new sales manager in town, so that position is filled and so you're promptly forgotten.

Unfortunately, most new sales managers don't know what they don't know. Why? Here's a "short list" of the various sales management issues and responsibilities you will encounter as the sales manager:

- Indentifying successful sales traits and behaviors so you can hire winners
- Establishing your new operating rhythm
- Setting standards of performance
- Identifying what's expected of you from your boss
- Making your expectations clear to the sales team
- Discovering the difference between leadership versus management
- Creating or maintaining a high performance culture
- Setting objectives
- Establishing/identifying leading indicators of success
- Interviewing
- Reference checking
- Coaching
- Counseling

- Disciplining
- Firing
- Motivating
- Demanding call reports
- Actually getting call reports on time if at all
- Reading call reports
- Managing expenses
- Compensating employees
- Training
- Giving recognition and praise
- Helping team members set goals
- Making projections
- Reporting up
- Disciplining
- Transitioning
- Balancing communication and personality styles
- Running effective meetings
- Delegating
- Routing
- Motivating
- Discussing pay as it relates to motivation
- Figuring out team dynamics
- Holding people accountable
- Forecasting
- Managing channels, partners, and alliances
- Managing growth and expectations

- Dealing with distance
- Reviewing wins and losses
- Managing people and processes
- Understanding and learning new technology
- Developing product, competitor, and customer knowledge
- Giving recognition in various ways:
  - Having employees in on matters and events
  - Giving them challenging work
  - Granting freedom and authority
- Reviewing performance
- Planning and executing course corrections
- Determining resource requirements and availability
- Evaluating strengths and weaknesses of team members, exploiting strengths, and shoring up weaknesses
- Getting buy in
- Conducting ride-alongs
- Holding office coaching sessions
- Dealing with difficult times
- Defining what *good* looks like
- Leading people through change
- Dealing with competitive pressure and pricing
- Determining market potential
- Managing relationships with accounts
- Dealing with the *prima donna* sales rep
- Developing a leadership style
- Teaching old dogs new tricks
- Creating a vision of a better future
- Getting to know your team

I'm guessing you're not up to speed on each and every one of these topics. Am I right?

According to David Snodgrass, director of sales for Windstream, a telephone and data firm, "That's right on target." Snodgrass admits, "We really don't do a good job of training sales managers." It's an unfortunate but widespread phenomenon: The bulk of small and midsized companies don't have good sales manager training. Most end up saying something like the following to new sales managers: "Go read this book" or "Find out what classes the local university offers." Or, they send these newbies to a traveling seminar when one passes through the area. But this approach leaves a big gap, and a lot of room for things to fall through the cracks.

You feel forgotten and alone, because in most cases you are. How's that for a reality check?

Here's your next one: Your new title is a misnomer. You aren't really managing sales: You are managing the people who make the sales, or at least the ones who take the orders.

You manage a lot of things, but sales isn't one of them. It might be easier to think in terms of managing the things that lead to sales—things like the number of first meetings your team gets, their ability to manage long sales cycles, and their aptitude for assessing customer problems and proposing customized solutions.

Or it might help to think of it this way: You can't really manage a fish, either. I learned that from my close buddy, Larry Claggett. We have known each other since elementary school; Larry was of the *trout specialist* for the Wisconsin Department of Natural Resources until he retired at the end of 2010.

I used to find it funny when I called him at work to set up a tee time for golf, and he answered his phone, "Fish Management, Larry speaking."

"How do you manage a fish?" I would joke.

But fish management is not a joke to Larry. Here's how he described what he does when I asked him for this book:

"Officially, I'm a cold water fisheries ecologist," Larry told me. I knew that once he mentioned *ecology* that we were going to be getting into a discussion of systems.

"So, what's on your radar?"

"I look at what's happening on the landscape, and how it affects trout and their habitat. We can't directly manage farm runoff, but we can participate with groups that do and lobby for changes. While our true authority starts at the stream bank or the lake shore, other events impact what's coming into the waters. To that end, we've shifted our focus to the watershed or large-scale landscape management, rather than just concentrating on what's in an individual stream or lake.

"The major efforts we make for trout are to bring about habitat changes that support the environment in which the fish live. It's more effective to manage the habitat than it is to deal with individual fish or species. Because fish can take care of themselves if we take care and protect the habitat."

In other words: Larry and his team manage the systems that affect the fish, and the fish take care of themselves.

And believe it or not—you are doing the same thing. You are managing the environment, culture, informal and formal systems, people, and processes of sales. Your efforts will have the same effect: The sales will take care of themselves when you take care of the salespeople and exhibit the right kind of leadership skills.

You're the sales manager, but you don't manage sales. Another way to look at it is this: You must coach the players to do what it takes to win instead of trying to coach the score.

Cliff Albert is Berry Plastics' Director of Sales for the Institutional Division. I asked him the same question I asked Larry. "What's on your radar?"

His response confirmed that sales management is really about being aware of all the little things that go into getting the order. In fact, Albert says, "Sales are a lagging indicator. If something is on the books, it has already happened and I can't influence it." Nonetheless, Albert looks at the numbers every day. "The first thing in the morning, I look at all year-to-date figures," he shares. "I look at dollars and I look at units. I look at it from a top line perspective. What are the business units doing? I look at it from a regional perspective. What are the sales guys' regions doing?

"Then I look at what our top five Strategic Accounts customers are doing. What are my top 10 gainers doing? What are my top 10 losers doing? That's my first snapshot. What I'm looking at is the overall. Where are we to budget? Where are we budgetwise to the year? Okay, we're here. We're a million dollars off budget. We have four months to make up a million bucks. How do we do that?"

Albert goes on to discuss the proactive stuff.

"I move on to the opportunities. I get into the CRM system and look at the selling stage to see what opportunities exist during the negotiation stage—because that's the last stage before you start celebrating the win. If you've sent pricing out, there's a greater opportunity there. So I sort my CRM to stages to see where we are and what we can do today to move these things through the pipeline. Then I can start making calls. And I can be a pain in the ass sometimes. I ask the people in the field, 'Hey what are these prospects thinking—and doing?'"

Cliff Albert continuously instructs his staff to "Respect the expiration date." In fact, it's almost a mantra for him: "[Putting] an expiration date on a proposal gives you license to call the customer every day for 30 days and ask what is going on. On day 29, you [let them know that] this proposal is expiring, and ask if they're going to make a decision. Opportunities are the leading indicator because closing those opportunities is what drives the sales report going forward.

"The third piece for me is how I help my team keep the process moving and make sure they are focusing on the right opportunities and next steps. Otherwise, they can be spinning like a hamster on a wheel. Are they focusing on the business and moving it forward? My time is best spent coaching them through the process.

"So, I'll call the guys and I'll ask for an overview of their territories. I want to know what's happening. You don't have to tell me you talked to Bob and he said this and we're having lunch next week. I don't care. You have to be able to give me a macro view of your region—top line, bottom line. Because if you're articulating all this detail, you're missing a lot of other touch points. You may be telling me about a $10,000 opportunity when a $1 million opportunity just went to a competitor.

I focus on pending and hot deals; I want my team to focus on these and know they will be asked about them. At the end of the week, we get on the phone together to share best practices and to try to understand what's happening within the regions."

Even though Albert knows the score, he doesn't manage it, and neither can you. You manage the people and coach them on the activities that put up the sales.

Albert manages a sales force and distributor network that is spread out all over the country. Although you may have a completely different kind of sales management job, his perspective is worth considering. Regardless of your particular situation, you can learn from his tactics and viewpoint. Sales are the lagging indicator; getting salespeople to do things that move sales forward is proactive sales management.

This book will help you develop a sales management philosophy, a set of beliefs about your job and the people you manage. It will also provide you with new skills and tools to bring to the job and help you implement your philosophy. You'll find forms, models, illustrations, and sales meeting exercises throughout. These are immediately applicable ideas that help you put this book into action. All of these tools (and more) are available in PDF format and downloadable at my web site: www.sparque.biz/AccidentalSM.

My ultimate goal is to challenge your thinking and introduce you to a wealth of new ideas to put into action. So, with that in mind, let's get started.

I often remark at the beginning of one of my live presentations, "I hope you like what I have to say, but it's okay if you don't. I'm a seminar leader not a stand up comedian. (I thought about being a stand up comedian, but I didn't want to work nights.) I'm here for your improvement, not for your enjoyment."

You don't know how good a seminar on sales management or a book on sales management is until you put some of the ideas into action.

To know and not to DO is not to know.

So I hope you like the book, but I also want to make you uncomfortable enough to examine your approach to the job and make some changes and refinements in what you're doing.

CHAPTER 1

Gnawing Your Way Out of the Sales Management Trap

A paradox is a statement that is seemingly contradictory or opposed to common sense yet is true. In *13 Fatal Errors Managers Make and How to Avoid Them,* Steven W. Brown describes the paradox of management: "You get paid for doing *less* of what you got promoted for doing *more* of." Top-producing salespeople who become sales managers often find themselves doing two jobs, their old one and their new one. The boss announces your promotion by saying something like this:

"Congratulations, you're the new sales manager. Of course, we want you to maintain your accounts until you've developed a couple of people to take them over."

That's how the *sales management trap* is sprung. You got promoted for being a good salesperson. But now you you get paid for doing less of what you got promoted for doing more of. It is next to impossible to find the time to develop salespeople to replace the irreplaceable *you* while you are still doing the job from which you were just promoted. And even if you manage to avoid doing your (prior) full-time sales job, you can quickly get trapped in the minutiae of sales management. These Stage 2 sales management tasks rob you of focus and time; they keep you busy, and send you home tired.

You walk in the front door and the person you love greets you affectionately.

"Hi, honey, how was your day?"

"Busy."

"Oh, so you got a lot done?"

"No, I didn't get anything done. I put out one fire after another."

Sound familiar?

Let's look at why this happens in case after case. There are four phases of learning any skill (bear with me, even if you've seen this model before). Let's look at how you learned to sell, for example. You started way back as a **Phase 1— Unconscious Incompetent** individual. At this phase, you don't know that you don't know. You're new to the job of sales. You can't imagine that it could be that hard. You're ready to go out and start making calls. It's great to be employed and starting a new career. Then, you run smack dab into Phase 2.

Phase 2—Conscious Incompetence. You know you don't know. Salespeople in this phase are hit with the complexity of the sales job. You are starting to hear objections and field complaints from customers, and are becoming aware that you don't know enough to succeed. The competition is fierce, and the customers are tough. How do you build relationships with people who won't take your calls? How can you sell your product without heavy discounting? You begin to wonder if you should join the military; it's got to be easier than this. Not every salesperson makes it through Phase 2, but those who do enter Phase 3, which is a very nice place to hang out.

Phase 3—Conscious Competence. This is the point in your sales career when you *know* that you know what you're doing. After a few years and hundreds of meetings, you are fully aware of what to expect. You're experienced, glib, and confident. You have a repeatable sales process that you have honed over the years. You have customers who buy from you more or less habitually, and you have been around long enough to have developed a network. They return your calls and refer you to their peers. Your career is on track, which leads you into the last phase.

Phase 4—Unconscious Competence. In this phase, you actually *forget* you know and just do it. You're operating on autopilot. You don't have to think about everything. The job is familiar and as natural to you as breathing. You are selling up a storm, just like I was. And the people in the corner offices have you on their radar for a promotion.

And that, my friend, is just about the time that your boss brings you the good news. You've been promoted!

If you accept that promotion, you will be a Phase 1 Sales Manager. You have now gone from a Phase 4 salesperson to a new manager who once again doesn't know how much he doesn't know. That's because you can't start a new job that requires a completely different skill set from the job you have been doing so well without going back through the phases of learning that will guide you through the new facets of sales *management*.

Here's the real rub. As the new sales manager, you have forgotten what you know about selling. You are skipping steps that a brand new person cannot skip. You take shortcuts because you can. But you may be managing salespeople who don't know they don't know. This is why developing salespeople can be so frustrating. Doesn't it sound fun?

Certainly not. In fact, it's not fun at all. But it is, of course, necessary. And that is why I am going to guide you through this process—and show you how to succeed at sales management more quickly than you would have if you weren't reading this book.

That's all; but that's plenty.

Jeff Sleete is the vice president of marketing for Sinclair Broadcasting. He describes the patience it takes to manage new people: "You can't get frustrated with people who don't know. You can never let that [get] old to you. They are going to have [the] same problems that the last person had, but you can't let that get old. They are going to fall down and make mistakes. You can't be irritated with them unless you want to crush their egos."

You don't want to crush egos or make people afraid to raise their hands and ask for help. So, acknowledge the fact that you will have to guide and coach new salespeople through all four phases of their development. Your key objective as a sales manager is to get sales results through others. It involves planning, staffing, training, leading, directing, and disciplining your salespeople. It means holding them accountable to achieve the results your company needs. As their boss, you have the most immediate and profound impact on their success and failure. But many sales managers have trouble finding enough time to do that developmental *people* stuff. They get trapped in the minutiae of their jobs. And trust me—there is plenty of minutiae.

This is why I've created the Sales Management Trap—a useful model you can use to isolate the tasks and duties that are mission critical from those that are not. (See Figure 1.1.) I call it a *trap* because new sales managers often get stuck in an endless cycle of Stage 1 and Stage 2 activities. These tasks eat up so much of their days that the sales manager doesn't spend enough time in Stage 3 tasks. For that reason, much of this book will focus on Stage 3 tasks—because the people side of the business is where the fun and freedom come in. Once you have a team of people who can sell (almost) as well as you could, you will end up hitting your numbers and spend more time celebrating success than putting out fires.

This book will move you from captivity to freedom.

Don't get me wrong, dealing with Stage 1 and 2 tasks are neither inherently bad nor inherently good. And sometimes they are urgent and necessary. However, when sales managers don't spend adequate time doing Stage 3 tasks, they don't

Stage 1	Stage 2	Stage 3	Stage 4
Nonmanagement Duties	**Other Management Tasks**	**Human Resource Development**	**Strategic Market Planning**
☐ Maintain status as top biller	☐ Sales support	☐ Staffing	☐ Strategic planning
☐ Handle own account list	☐ Account list management	☐ Training	☐ Market analysis
☐ Handle regional accounts	☐ Monitor sales	☐ Coaching/counseling	☐ Customer analysis
☐ Handle national accounts	☐ Conduct sales meetings	☐ Developing salespeople	☐ Competitive analysis
	☐ Firefighting	☐ Motivation	☐ Cost analysis
	☐ Handle complaints	☐ Communicating	☐ Profit management
	☐ Communicate with management	☐ Mentoring	☐ Forecast sales
	☐ Sales force compensation	☐ Recruiting	☐ Prepare budget
	☐ Inventory management		☐ Set objectives

Figure 1.1   The Sales Management Trap

multiply themselves and achieve results through others to the extent that they could.

Berry Plastic's Cliff Albert took one look at The Sales Management Trap and made the following comment:

> When you don't see success in the field, you are very quick to jump in and get your hands dirty—to the point where you're doing the lower level tasks that you've hired other folks to complete. You want to bypass the rep and call the customer yourself to find out where in the process the sale is. You've got a $2.5 million opportunity and it's sitting there staring at you while your sales guy is telling you that it's moving along. You want to call the customer and find out precisely, "Where is this project?" At Level 3, you're really coaching your team to understand that this project is not moving. Unless you resurrect it, it has flat lined—and you might as well move on to something else because you've exhausted every bit of life that's left in it.

Use The Sales Mangement Trap to see exactly where you're spending your sales management time and effort. When you are operating in Stage 1, you are a salesperson. When you are operating in Stage 2, you are managing—and while these tasks may be important, they don't help you grow as a manager. You've been putting out fires and handling complaints for years. Running a sales meeting to discuss pipeline progress and next month's special program is not the same as running one that's designed to develop your team's sales skills. Preparing budgets is a necessary evil, while coaching people is the surest way to *make* these budgets.

Even executives can get mired in minutiae: According to Matrix Fitness' Kent Stevens, Senior VP of Marketing:

> This is such a fast game. Every day goes by so quickly. I am not spending enough time sitting in a quiet room to gather my

thoughts about the big picture, asking myself what's going on, and really working on strategy. A lot of the job is reactive. I need to delegate the minutiae and spend more time leading the strategy on how we are going to continue growing this. I can get a call from a territory manager about a pricing issue or field a customer complaint about a shipping issue or incomplete order. Bigger issue items to me are things like dissecting our industry by account, by channel, even by product. I have to answer questions like, How can we sell more crank cycles? How can we develop a [more noticeable] presence in the 'active aging' market?

One of my weaknesses is that I have always been able to handle a lot of tasks. I need to better learn how to delegate the small stuff, and rid myself of the notion that I always need to be involved in every project and process, or that I always want to keep my e-mail box clean. We recently had back to back to back trade shows, which lead to countless e-mails piling up way above my comfort level. I realized that when I took a couple of days on the weekend to clear my inbox, I could delete the older ones quickly when I got to them—because they all involved matters that had taken care of themselves without my involvement. It helped me see that I don't always have to chime in on every situation; when I don't, people just do their jobs.

Like so many before him, brand new sales manager Garfield Ogilvie spent his early sales management career trapped doing Stage 1 and 2 tasks. Now a vice president of sales for Clear Channel Outdoor in Dallas, Texas, he was promoted from within to his first sales management post at a radio station in Timmons, Ontario. According to Ogilvie, "In the early going, I had to learn that my role was not to make the sales. It was to teach others how to do it. I had three salespeople in my first sales management job—and I was generating 60 to 70 percent of the revenue. Essentially, I had two people servicing the accounts so I could go out and make it rain someplace else. In short—I was doing their jobs for them."

In fact, Ogilvie didn't get out of the Sales Management Trap until he took a job in Toronto:

[There] I had a number of salespeople dispersed over a number of markets. I started to get away from making the sales to taking a more supervisory role—simply due to physical distance. Then, when I jumped back to a sales management job in another market and had a staff of 10, I realized that I had transitioned.

I had been promoted from within in the first situation. Because of this, I hired people to take care of accounts that I had nurtured and couldn't cut the ties. But I didn't have the personal history with the customers in the regional sales management job in Toronto that I previously had. So I made the transition and became more of a leader-manager. I went into that market without prior sales history. I went in as a manger; I didn't start as a salesperson. So I didn't have to get rid of existing relationships.

Without a sales history, I could build relationships on a sales management perspective. They weren't based on having dealt with an account list of 25 businesses that I knew intimately from selling and servicing them exclusively for a number of years. I met people in the new situation as a manager—so the dynamics of my role and relationships with customers were different. For me, it really required that physical location to make the transition.

Note that Ogilvie didn't make the full transition until he took a new sales management job. And of course, that is always an option. Ogilvie got stuck in Stage 1—generating 70 percent of the revenue. He didn't have a clear picture of what "good sales management" looks like. When he moved to Toronto, he was hired as a sales manager and not promoted from within. Mind you, it is possible to transition to higher level sales management tasks without resigning your current position even if you were promoted from within. It's not easier, but it is possible.

Ken Greenwood and I worked together for seven years conducting a quarterly Leadership Institute for high-level broadcast executives. Ken puts it in much the same way that Ogilvie does:

> It is more difficult when you are promoted to sales manager from within—since you're put in charge of the group of which you were once a member. It's easier to come in from the outside, begin to lead that group, and make the necessary adjustments—because there is less history involved. When you've been a playing member of the team, you know a lot of its members' shortcomings and frailties. But you may never have thought about their strengths. You only have half a view of the group of people you're now managing.

And it's hard because you're new to management, too.

Ogilvie's first position in sales management was difficult because he was trying to do both his old and his new job.

Successful sales management careers are built on Stage 3— or Human Resource Development—activities. Nothing you've done up until this point in your sales career has prepared you to excel at these skills. Once you master them, you're well on your way to becoming a successful sales manager.

Focusing and spending time in Stage 3 Sales Management Tasks is where you make your career. Getting stuck in Stage 1 and 2 makes your life a living hell of constant firefighting. Stage 3 sales management tasks allow you to multiply yourself and your expertise through others. Otherwise, you will spend your time doing your salespeople' jobs for them and constantly cleaning up their messes.

The number one threat to your career as a sales manager occurs when you diminish your impact by failing to develop your team to be at *least* as good as you were when you were simply selling.

The *secret* of sales management success is to get so good at Stage 3 and 4 tasks that you don't have to spend huge amounts of time on Stage 1 and Stage 2 tasks. You generate all of your leverage as a manager at these higher levels. These are the management responsibilities that lead to big sales increases.

In other words: **You will have better salespeople when you become a better sales manager.**

A salesperson approached me once during a seminar break and said, "Everything you're saying makes sense, Chris—except I've got a terrible account list."

"Then you're probably not a very good salesperson," I said.

"What do you mean?" he replied, somewhat offended.

"If you were a better salesperson, you would have been able to turn some of those terrible prospects into good customers. If you were a great salesperson, your management would have entrusted better customers to your care."

It is easy for salespeople to blame their lack of production on management, the competition or the situation, rather than take a hard look at their own shortcomings in knowledge, skills, and attitude. The same goes for sales managers. You can complain about your salespeople, but when you become a better boss you have better people. It never fails.

Sales and sales management are two completely different jobs that require two completely different mental approaches. That's why the transition is difficult for many people to make—and for some, it never occurs.

In fact, some of the characteristics that made you a great salesperson and got you promoted to sales manager will actually work *against* you as a sales manager. The next chart looks at just eight traits. I cut this out of a magazine many years ago, have referred to it often, and have even added my own embellishments over the years.

Salesperson	Sales Manager
1. Drives self	Finds out what drives his team and uses that
2. Feels a constant sense of urgency to sell	Practices patience and uses pressure sparingly
3. Wants and gets recognition	Gives recognition and often gets very little in return
4. Lone Ranger (self-reliant)	Relies on team
5. Builds customer relationships and loyalty	Builds relationships with team and fosters loyalty to the company
6. Perseveres	Cuts losses quickly
7. Nonconformist and freelancer	Sets standards (works by the book)
8. Doer	Organizer/strategist/coach/facilitator

This is a very tough transition to make, and not every new sales manager makes it.

Because, as the aforementioned paradox states, you are paid to do less of what you were promoted for doing more of. Because you are already good at selling and your natural tendency is to gravitate back toward what you are good at. While Stage 2 sales management tasks are necessary, they have a tendency to consume so much time that you don't develop your people. And employees who aren't coached and developed are great at starting fires—leaving you to put them out.

And you're trapped.

And that's where this book comes in. I focus on the sales management task and behaviors that will get you out of the Sales Management Trap and bring more meaning and satisfaction to the job.

Here are a five ways to plot your escape from Stage 1 and 2 sales management tasks to the higher level and higher leverage ones:

Escape Mechanism 1: Plan Higher Level Tasks First

Plan your week by scheduling Stage 3 tasks first, and setting aside time to coach and train your people. Talk to your boss about one or two items in Stages 3 and 4, and make these activities a priority. There will be even more fires to fight if you don't make time to coach and develop your salespeople.

Escape Mechanism 2: Quit Fighting Fires You Didn't Start

When complications do arise, don't immediately jump in to save the day for your salespeople. Instead, encourage your employees to come up with a game plan for solving their own problems. Then, let them execute the plan. This teaches your salespeople how to prevent and put out their own fires in the future, while freeing up more time for you to complete Stage 3 and 4 tasks. Yes, I know you can fix it for them. But doing so teaches them to bring you more problems to solve and do even more of their jobs for them. (See "Who's Managing Whom?")

Escape Mechanism 3: Get On the Same Page as Your Boss

Your boss needs to be to be clear about what's expected of you. Does your boss see the importance of developing the sales team while achieving this quarter's sales results? Or is hitting the number the only thing that matters? Does the boss expect you to be the top producer and the sales manager? Does the boss plan to coach you through your transition or are you on your own? Has the boss done your job before so that you can tap into some tribal wisdom? Are there things on the sales management trap form that the boss wants you doing more of, less of, or none of? I'm guessing your boss wants you to do everything on the list. What you want to do is manage expectations and find out which five to seven things are most important to him.

After all, it is impossible to meet expectations if you don't know what they are. The Sales Management Trap is a mechanism to help you have a very focused conversation that answers the question, "What's my job? And how am I doing at it?"

And that might be a good thing to know, don't you think?

Escape Mechanism 4: Don't Get Too Attached to Your Desk

Get out into the field with your salespeople. You'll be able to coach and develop them better once you've observed them in action. Before a critical customer meetings, go over the salesperson's pre-meeting plan; then review the meeting based on the plan and the results. *This* is what coaching is all about. Don't be tempted to let them wing it and then bail them out—or worse, chew them out in the car after the meeting. I have always found it better to coach before the call so I can influence the outcome rather than do a *post mortem* on everything that went wrong.

Escape Mechanism 5: Cultivate the Right Relationships

Understand the following major working relationships for the salespeople and sales managers. Salespeople succeed by spending time with these people in this order: (1) Customers; (2) Managers; (3) Colleagues. Sales *managers*, on the other hand, succeed by spending time with these people in this order: (1) Subordinates; (2) Superiors; (3) Customers; (4) Colleagues.

Who's Managing Whom?

Believe it or not, many of your salespeople will come to you and ask you to do their jobs for them. That's a trap.

Jim Lobaito—founder and president of The Performance Group in Des Moines, Iowa—describes how he gnawed his way out of the Sales Management Trap and made the transition without having to change locations:

> I learned the hard way that there is a difference between generating revenue—what a salesperson does—and driving revenue—a sales manager's responsibility. I vividly remember the exact moment when I made the transition from a salesperson who managed people to a sales manager. It was 5:05 P.M., and a salesperson stopped by my office and said, "Now don't forget, you said you would get this done for me tomorrow." She threw it on my desk, and I replied, "Of course, yes."
>
> She proceeded out the door. [All of a sudden, it was] seven o'clock at night, and I looked up to realize that I was the only person left in the building that night—the only one worried about whether or not we were going to hit our revenue mark. At that point, I said, "That's it. I will no longer be the only

person who cares about these matters. I am going to share my worry with every single other team member." And that became the pivotal event [that prompted me to make] the transition to becoming a sales manager the very next day.

I can go close any [deal for my salespeople; however, if] that's all a sales manager is going to do, then you force the whole organization to depend on you—and you don't really develop your people. So I had to figure out how to drive revenue into the organization through my sales team and not *myself*.

The first thing I stared to do was to stop taking on more than I could handle. I quit being accommodating [and acting like] I was the only person who could [get certain things done]. [People who] first get into management [tend to] carry over the rugged individualism or Lone Ranger salesperson mentality— that attitude that I will do everything myself, and do it to perfection. But you have to get over that and accept the fact that if your team does it to 80 percent of the level that you can do it, that's still better than the team across town; and so good enough becomes good enough. You get paid for movement and progress. You don't get paid for perfection. I made the mental adjustment to say, "No, I don't need to touch this [about certain topics]."

The second thing I did [was to] start making [my expectations of my employees] very tangible [and apparent] by posting them. I called a meeting the next day and said, "When your call reports come in, we're going to post them the next day." There was a lot of resistance [but people really had no choice].

I acknowledged that people weren't happy, but I told them that the most competitive people keep score—and so we were going to keep track of activities, [since I knew this would] lead to results.

We started monitoring our activities, and the team got comfortable with that. [The next initiative I had to establish was to get them to] start tracking the results. Then, [we'd have to begin] raising expectations.

[I made the] transition over time [by continuously] asking myself, "What am I struggling with that I don't need to be?"

And, "How can I make this more tangible for the team and measure it?" And, "How can I create a structure with which I can run it without being overwhelmed?"

Lobaito started posting numbers and keeping score of the things that lead to results. He learned the vital lesson that you cannot coach the score of the game; you can only coach the things that lead to scoring.

It is very hard to change unless you are brutally honest about what is currently happening and what has to change to take your career to a higher level. Use the Sales Management Trap over the next 30, 60, and 90 days to identify what items and tasks are taking up your time and attention, what you need to be doing more of, and finally, what you want to be doing *less* of. To help you in this endeavor, there is a PDF of the Sales Management Trap available at www.AccidentalSalesManager .com/forms. From here, you can download it, print it, and post it on your bulletin board or into your paper planning system. You can then use it on a regular basis to estimate how much time you spend on each task, and to imagine what might happen if you spent more time on the Stage 3 and Stage 4 activities.

It is hard to change a behavior until you are aware of it. Simply by noticing you spent a day doing Stage 1 and 2 activities is a start. Once you are aware that you are not getting results through others, you can consciously decide to plan a Stage 3 management task for tomorrow.

That's your job.

How are you doing?

Too many new sales managers take way too long to get the kind of job clarity laid out in The Sales Management Trap tool. You don't have to be one of them.

CHAPTER 2

Fourteen Lessons You Won't Have to Learn the Hard Way

L et's start with the assumption that they made you the sales manager because you were the best person for the job. You're smart. You're interpersonally astute. You have good instincts. And you're probably doing 85 or 90 percent of the job correctly already. What you may *not* have is formal management training or the language to describe some of the management moves you make.

You may be doing the right things, but not know why they are the right things. This chapter will fix much of that.

Every sales manager I interviewed shared stories and insights about the lessons they had learned about sales management the hard way. We learn so much more from our failures and setbacks than we do from our successes. When everything is going well, we think we are bullet proof. When things go wrong, we have to stop and examine what happened and what we could have done differently.

We'll get to those in just a moment. But while we're on the topic of learning things the hard way, here's your . . .

Instant Sales Meeting Idea:
Orienting the New Hire

One way for a new *salesperson* to get to know the other salespeople on the team is to have each salesperson tell the newbie what he or she learned about selling for your company the *hard way*. Here are a few ways to phrase this question:

1. What do you wish you had known about selling for our company on the first day you started?

2. What did you have to find out about selling the
   hard way?
3. What is the best advice you can give our new team member to get her off to a positive start?

Salespeople generally like to share their opinions. The first
time you do this exercise, brief the team and ask them not to
terrify their new colleague with horror stories. At the same
time, let them know that a little self-disclosure is a good
thing.

When I asked sales managers what they learned the hard
way, they had no trouble vividly recalling their own teachable
moments.

You likely hear a lot of pundits talk about *teachable moments*.
The term was popularized by Robert Havighurst in his schol-
arly work, *Human Development and Education*. In the context
of educational theory, Havighurst explains,

> A developmental task is a task which is learned at a specific
> point and which makes achievement of succeeding tasks
> possible. When the timing is right, the ability to learn a par-
> ticular task will be possible. This is referred to as a "teachable
> moment." It is important to keep in mind that unless the time
> is right, learning will not occur. Hence, it is important to
> repeat important points whenever possible so that when a
> student's teachable moment occurs, s/he can benefit from
> the knowledge.

All of us are most susceptible to soul searching, coaching
and course correction *after* we have had a setback or failure.
We are much more open to help when we feel frightened,
embarrassed, or vulnerable than when we feel on top of the
world and invincible.

What follows are are hard lessons, but learning them makes your job a lot easier going forward. And learning them from people who have gone before you will speed up your sales management success.

Hard Lesson #1: Trust Your Instincts from Day One and Act on Them Quickly

Alert sales managers act at the first small sign of trouble. According to Berry Plastics' director of sales, Cliff Albert,

> Every new manager learns you need to make decisions a lot faster. When you think there is an issue, it means there is an issue—one you need to act upon. Ultimately, a team is only successful when all parts are running [correctly]. If you have one part that is running slower than the others, you must try to fix it. If you [realize] that it can't be fixed, you need to act. Firing people is the worst part of our jobs. But a lot of times, that person who is holding the rest of the team back becomes a cancer and influences some good people into bad behavior. In short: Act fast. Think through things. But when you *think* you might have a problem, you should know that you most likely already have that problem.

That doesn't mean you do something arbitrarily. You will probably want to check in with your boss and tell her what you're thinking and what you want to do. But act.

Hard Lesson #2: Firing an Underperforming Salesperson Is Usually a Relief for Both of You

Kent Stevens of Matrix Fitness echoes this sentiment as he reflects on how agonizing it was the first time he fired a salesperson.

You're not going to be able to save everybody. You are trying to be a coach or teacher—to get people to be the best they can be. You put a lot of hard work and passion into it. Sometimes you simply have to cut bait. This was the hardest lessons for me to learn—and firing someone for the first time was one of the most difficult things I ever had to do. So much so that I held onto that person much longer than I should have; I mean, about a year too long. I thought that eventually he was going to be more motivated; I thought he'd see the people, do the report and understand when to listen to the customer. But I finally realized that my job was to grow my company, and that there might be a better job for this person somewhere else. It is usually a not a surprise to the person you fire. In this case, the employee stayed calm and asked about next steps—making it a relief for both of us (and making me wonder why I waited so long to do it).

The sales rep probably wondered the same thing. Being fired rarely surprises a sales rep, nor should it. In many cases, it's a relief for them, because failing is never fun. Being fired may be exactly the wake-up call they need to relaunch their career with a new company. Meanwhile, you have a new rep you're excited about developing.

Hard Lesson #3: Salespeople Always Rebel Against "The Boss"

Richard Williams, the regional manager for the Western Region for Radio Network in New Zealand, didn't hesitate for a moment when I asked about learning sales management the hard way:

Every sales manager has gone through that phase where you're a salesperson, you're an account manager, and you're a senior salesperson. And then you find yourself in that office in the corner—and you're the new manager of that sales team you used to be on. And someone hands you a few bits and pieces of information. They give you some records. And tell you what reports you've got to do. But then you have to do this wonderful thing of managing people.

The hardest thing I had to learn was that the authoritarian style only works for awhile. You learn very quickly that although you may have the title and people will obey you at first, they will rebel after a very short time. The lesson I learned was that inclusiveness works better as a managing style. Getting salespeople involved in the decision-making that affected them created more buy-in. But it didn't happen all at once. In fact, I didn't realize that until I had a few people walk out the door.

Once I started seeing my role as a leader and not a manager, things changed. I began to realize that my job wasn't just to *be the boss*; it was to develop people to their full potential. And there are a lot of things that go into that. It requires looking at each person individually to understand their goals and how to manage them. I learned quickly that I couldn't manage everyone in the same way—and I became a coach.

You can manage a function, but you coach people.

Not a bad mantra for the Accidental Sales Manager. Choosing a leadership style consciously is important. We'll spend more time on your options Hard Lesson #5. For now, the lesson to latch onto is that just barking orders rarely works for long. Asking questions and listening is the answer to many sales management problems.

Hard Lesson #4: Share Control and Let Salespeople Buy In

Tim McMahon is the Clinical Associate Professor of Marketing at Creighton University in Omaha, NE; he has also worked in senior-level marketing positions in two Fortune 100 companies. He describes an entrepreneurial venture of his own in which he acquired the company and walked in with dozens of ideas for changing things.

> I learned that rather than try to control behavior, you can actually nurture and guide it. [Political consultant and author] Frank Luntz said the real secret to persuasion is inducing people to persuade themselves. A lot of salespeople have a spirit [that] drives them. We hire people who have a strong ego drive. But then we proceed to tell them exactly what to do and micromanage them into the dirt [and suppress their] egos, [and then] they get angry and start to divert their energy into non-productive activities.

Bob Pike, does seminars for people who do seminars and other training. He says, "People rarely resist their own ideas." When people pursue their own ideas with passion and energy, all the sales manager has to do is get out of the way.

Hard Lesson #5: Your Salespeople Will Have Problems That Paralyze Them (Temporarily) and You Will Hear About Them

The *people* side of the business can be messy. As one VP told me, "I wish I had known how to diaper 10 or 12 salespeople when I started. Everyone has different needs and you have to learn how to manage them differently."

Windstream's Snodgrass puts it this way:

> The tough one I find for myself and other managers is you are always going to have individual problems with someone on the team. It can be something with their family, or a personal

financial or health issue. With experience, you learn how to deal with those issues. I just advise new sales managers to expect them. These problems [will exist] no matter what kind of team you have, young or experienced; they're predicaments that affect high-income and average reps alike. I wish there were a class I had taken earlier in my career to become more skillful at handling those personal issues, and that there were better guidelines on how much to counsel employees. How far do you go getting to know them personally rather than keeping the relationship strictly business? Even though you frequently tend to rely on HR, they may not have the depth to help you in midsize companies.

Some of the questions that will run through your mind from time to time are as follows: *Why can't my salespeople be more like me when I was in sales?*, *Why don't they have my drive and my confidence?*, and *Why don't they have my work ethic?* There is a very simple answer to those questions—one that will keep you from ever asking or thinking about them again.

Because they aren't you.

You may be able to compartmentalize your problems. You worry about problems at home when you're at home and can do something about them. But others bring all of their worries to work. Giving them a sympathetic ear and helping them structure and restructure their day can help refocus them on the job. There are times where your counseling skills aren't up to the problems they bring you. You can refer them to resources inside and outside of your company so they can get the help they need.

But understand that counseling is the act of advising people on personal problems. Coaching is helping them overcome sales problems. These are two different skill sets.

Hard Lesson #6: Become Conscious of Your Leadership Style Early

Most sales managers become the boss before they have developed a philosophy of leadership. All of a sudden, they have a business card that says *Sales Manager* on it and they have to start being the boss, whatever that means.

Be careful.

Most new managers find the easiest (and most natural) thing to do is choose a leadership style by default. For example, *I like the way one boss ran sales meetings so I'll use that.* Or, *I will never yell at people in the hallway like that boss did.* You have been observing other managers for a while so you "steal" parts of their act that seem to fit yours.

You take bits and pieces from the good and bad bosses you worked for and cobble them together. Your leadership style emerges on the fly without a lot of thought. The obvious problem is that you may not have had enough good examples to fill your leadership tool kit.

One way to think of your leadership style is as a continuum from autocratic to democratic. An autocratic boss shouts orders and lays down the law. He or she sets standards and reads people the riot act when they don't comply. Compliance is more important to autocrats than commitment. "Get the job done," is their mantra. This in-your-face type of manager tends to do well with new people who are still afraid of him and with workers who require a lot of structure to succeed.

Of course, the autocratic boss drives away people who want to have some control of their work and apply their own ideas to solving sales problems. On the other side of the continuum, the democratic or inclusive boss is always trying to get buy-in for the goals and input on important decisions from his team. At the very far end of the scale—and the complete opposite of an autocratic leader—is the delegator. The delegator's approach is akin to, "I trust you to get the job done and tell me when it's finished. I'm here to support you if you need me, but you know how to get results. Go for it."

Maybe you can see where I'm going with this. There are times to be autocratic and times to be democratic. When you are in the midst of a downturn, you need to be more hands on and inspect activities more closely. When you have an experienced sales team, you can loosen the controls and ask them to tell you how they are going to make their numbers instead of you telling them how to do it.

Think of it this way: Depending on the situation and the person, you can lead by telling, selling (persuading people why they need to do something), asking, or simply acting in an advisory capacity when someone comes to you. Ultimately, these are choices you make every day with your individual team members. Making them consciously instead of by default is the mark of a seasoned manager.

Here's what I mean by acting "consciously." Say an experienced salesperson comes to you with a problem. You can solve it or assume the role of coach. If you choose coaching, you become a bit more detached from the outcome. Imagine, gazing off into space, taking a puff of your imaginary pipe, exhaling and saying, "That's an interesting dilemma you've presented. What do you think you can do to work your way though it?" Listen and guide the person with questions so that she comes up with a solution she owns. Giving the problem back to veterans is usually a good practice. Ken Greenwood would call this a *high support style*, you're supporting your salesperson, but asking her to come up with the right answer.

But using the same tact with a rookie, might overwhelm him. You can be more autocratic and say something like,

"There are two things I want you to do this afternoon. First, call the customer and say . . .

This is what Ken Greenwood calls a high direct style.

You may already be doing this unconsciously. Now you know why it works.

Hard Lesson #7: Your Salespeople Want to Please You So Much They Will Tell You What They Think You Want to Hear

If you tend to be an autocratic leader or you have a problem with losing your temper, you may intimidate people— something that might compel them to feel as though they have to hide things from you. Of course, if you yell at great people, they will either laugh at you or find a better boss. That said, there must be plenty of bad bosses whose salespeople are afraid to tell them what is *really* happening.

The November 15, 2010, issue of the *Chicago Tribune* had a special section on the city's top workplaces. As I thumbed through the "Exclusive List of the Top 100 Places to Work," I found the section where employees in the survey also got to add comments. Here are five statements made by employees about their companies:

1. "I have many opportunities to learn and grow at this organization."
2. "I get the formal training I want for my career."
3. "I feel genuinely appreciated at this organization"
4. "My manager listens to me."
5. And finally, the one that jumped off the page at me: "It's easy to tell my boss the truth."

Look at that list and see how little is required to make your department a place where people love to work. Every single one of those things is within your control and requires virtually no budget, especially if you take on the training burden. (And sales training is too important to leave to the training department anyway.) Why *shouldn't* it be easy to tell your manager the truth? I know sometimes the boss doesn't like to hear bad news, but keeping bad news hidden is not the way for an organization to succeed.

As my late colleague Norm Goldsmith used to say, "Would you rather have an employee come to you with a smoldering ember or a raging forest fire?"

Your reaction to mistakes and lost sales will determine how open and honest salespeople will be with you.

I'm not a shouter. Sure, I have rolled my eyes on a few too many occasions, but I don't embarrass people in front of others. And I genuinely want them to improve. But one thing I learned the hard way is that salespeople want to please the boss too much.

I can remember a time when I was a manager, and a salesperson came into the office at 4:30 P.M. He walked quickly past my door. He had driven 112 miles north to make a call on a prospect.

"Hey Michael," I called to him.

He poked his head around the door and looked in my office.

"Come in," I said to him. "How was your meeting today?"

"Great," he said, smiling. "It was a great meeting."

"So you got an order, then?"

"Not yet. It was a first meeting."

"I know that, but you said it was 'great.' What made it great if you didn't get an order?"

"Well, we talked for an hour and a half."

"So he didn't throw you out."

"In fact, he really likes the way we deliver our content and thinks we're onto something."

"What's the next step, Michael?"

"He wants me to call him in the spring."

"It's October. Spring is six months from now. And the entire season is 92 days long. Do you have a day in the spring when he wants you to call?"

"No. He just said that he wants me to call him in the spring."

"So let me ask you again. How was the meeting that you just drove 112 miles to and 112 miles back from?"

"Terrible?"

"Use words that mean something, Michael. It was a *continuation*. You didn't make a sale and you don't have a next step on a certain date. That's a continuation or a non-win. There's nothing wrong with not closing. Nobody closes every sale. The mistake you are making is calling a meeting in which nothing positive happened a 'great meeting.'"

Salespeople like Michael are hooked on *hopium*. They present and pray hoping they have done enough to win the business. And their sales process ends there.

Your job is to give them a reality check—to help them look at failure as part of the process and not something to be ashamed of or worried about. What you want from your salespeople is honest communication. You want them to use language that describes what actually transpires.

Failing to foster the kind of relationship where salespeople can tell you the truth can lead to some dire consequences. Consider my conversation with Michael. If I had taken him at his word that it was a "great meeting," I would have asked some entirely different questions—and possibly received some less-than-accurate answers. These answers would have ended up in our sales projections and made those projections filled with hopium.

Here's what could have happened had I gone with the "great meeting" scenario.

"How many salespeople do they have that they want to train, Michael?"

"Thirty-eight, but they will be at 50 in the spring."

"Do they want to train them all?"

"That's what he was talking about."

"How certain are you that this will close in the spring?"

"I'd rate it at 70 percent minimum."

"I'll put it in at 60 percent for now. Good work, Michael."

Now, I have a six-figure order in one of our sales pipelines that has no next step, and no real business being in the pipeline. That's at least a partial explanation for why Chief Sales Officer Insights reports 54 percent of the deals that are projected as at least 75 percent sure to close never do. Your people are blowing the sweet smelling smoke of *hopium* your way. If you're not careful, you will readily inhale it, and continue to blow it up the line.

Don't. Ask questions. Make sure that a "great meeting" means the same thing to your salespeople as it does to you.

Hard Lesson #8: Your Salespeople May Not Want to Hear What Their Prospects Really Think So They Don't Ask

Michael told me what he thought I wanted to hear. And maybe he heard what he wanted to hear. ("This customer is going to buy in the spring") This is not unique. Be on guard against it.

Berry Plastic's Cliff Albert offers the following insight:

What ends up happening is [that] a salesperson can be seduced by a large piece of business in his pipeline. Sometimes they are hands-off because they like to see a $2.5 million opportunity just sitting there in the pipeline. They don't push it—because if they do, it might go away—and so goes their hope. I've seen situations [in which salespeople] are forced by management to ask the tough questions—(1) "When are you making a decision?," [and] (2) "When are you doing such and such?" They find out that my wonderful prospect or opportunity has actually been talking to my competitor. Now all of a sudden, there is a rejuvenation from that salesperson who realizes, *I'm about to lose this*. These kinds of opportunities can be renewed when the salesperson gets a sense of urgency and realizes that [they're about to lose such a fruitful] opportunity.

You have to ask your salespeople the tough questions. Otherwise, they may never ask their prospects the tough questions.

Kent Stevens asserts the following:

All salespeople need to ask the tough questions and actually *listen* to the answers. When they don't, they're always somehow surprised that they don't close opportunities they have in the pipeline. Stop wasting time on low-probability opportunities. Instead, ask the hard question: "Is there anything that would prevent you with placing an order with us right now?" A lot of salespeople want to tiptoe around that, but I think it's a fair question. I know we're not going to get every deal, but at least we can try to improve if we know why we're *not* getting them.

Does your sales team know that losing a piece of business is not the end of the world? Or do they get a double whammy every time they lose a deal. The prospect tells them "No," and then their sales manager piles on because their prospect says no.

It's tough enough to lose the business. Salespeople who lose in the field don't need to be made to feel like even bigger losers when they get back to the shop.

Hard Lesson #9: To Surpass Old Limits, You Need Higher Standards, But Develop Them from the Ground Up Instead of Dictating Them

Successful sales organizations have high standards of performance. But most companies have wishes instead of standards.

Whenever I talk with a sales manager who says, "I wish my salespeople would be more proactive." Or, "I wish my salespeople would do more new business development," I know I am dealing with a wisher instead of a standard setter.

Standards are measurable indicators of performance involving consequences for noncompliance.

If you can influence standards in your unit, all the better. If you are in a larger corporate setting, you may experience a corporate VP getting involved with setting standards for your team.

Do you take dictation? Neither do your salespeople. But that doesn't stop managers from dictating standards from on high.

The corporate higher ups at one particular company with whom I worked had dictated to every sales manager that their salespeople had to make a minimum of 15 calls a week—and each of those calls had to be face-to-face.

"How many calls do *you* think we should be making, Chris?" one sales manager asked me. "Because my team members are having a very hard time getting 15 legitimate face-to-face meetings a week."

"How far from budget are you right now?" I asked.

"We're off 7 percent year-on-year."

"So you want to close that gap."

"Well yes; that would make corporate a lot happier."

"On average, how many face-to-face calls were your sales-people actually making before corporate made 15 the new standard?"

In case you missed it, the most important word in the last sentence is *actually*. What is *actually* happening is what is getting you the result that is 7 percent below your goal.

The sales manager answered, "Everybody gets at least seven face-to-face calls a week. Some get to nine. Occasionally, someone will have a bad week and only get four or five."

"So all corporate wants people to do is to *double their call rates*, when you're 7 percent from goal?" I asked. (Imposing standards without knowing what's actually happening can demoralize managers and salespeople.)

"Uh-huh."

"And you're halfway through the year. So let's up the call rate 14 percent, since you only have half the year to make up the 7 percent shortfall. That means a person who is making seven calls a week needs to make 0.98 more—let's say one more call to get to eight Now that's 50 calls a year times per rep multiplied by your your 12 reps—and that gives you 600 more calls. Do you think you could sell that up the line?"

"I think I have to try or lose my team."

The story makes a very clear point: Until you know what is actually happening, setting a standard is a counterproductive, monumental waste of time.

Hard Lesson #10: Without Standards There Is No Discipline

As I write this, Kentucky basketball coach John Calipari is in the sports news because he yelled at one of his players and obviously swore as he was doing so. I would never tell you to swear at a salesperson, but I will tell you that you have to confront negative behavior and correct them more than occasionally. If you and your team don't have standards to shoot for, then every confrontation becomes personal instead of instructive.

And "instructive" is the key word in the last sentence.

Let's revisit our sales manager who has gotten the call rate reduced from 15 to eight per week. He is determined to hold salespeople to this standard he has renegotiated with his boss. Two weeks into the "new way of doing business," salesperson Mary's child falls ill, and she misses two days of work. Consequently, her call report shows just four calls in three full days of selling.

Is this a discipline problem, or a personal problem?

That is a question you need to ask. In this case, it's a personal issue. You do not have to meet with Mary to read her the riot act about her lack of commitment to the cause and the importance of pulling her weight despite the adversity at home. But if next week Mary works five days and still only manages four calls, then you have one of those teachable moments. And remember: You are in coaching mode, not punishment mode. You have a discipline interview.

"Mary, can I have a word with you?"

"Sure. What's up?"

"Well, I noticed that you made four calls last week; we had agreed that eight is the number we're now shooting for. Can you tell me what happened?

"Sorry. I had to put the finishing touches on that major presentation. It's a $500,000 deal and I wanted it to be perfect."

"And I agree—that deal is important. At the same time, I want to show progress toward the standard. And I want you back on track. That means that I need you back to eight meetings over the next three weeks. Nine would be even better; that way, you'll be back to par and erase the deficit within four weeks."

"Wow. I don't think I can erase it in four weeks."

"Well, it's one extra meeting every two days. Can you do it in six weeks?"

"I'll try."

"Do you remember what Yoda told Luke Skywalker?"

"I wasn't alive when *Star Wars* came out. Do you have some better movie references?"

"Sorry, this is a good one. He said, 'Do or do not. There is no try.' I want to know you'll comply with this, even if you're not wild about it. I'm having this meeting with you and one other person who's behind. I don't want to be having it."

"Are you going to fire me if I don't do it?"

"While that's always an option, we're a long way from that."

"I don't want that."

"Neither do I, Mary. Let's talk about a more positive future. What has to happen for you to get eight face-to-face calls this week and next? What would you have to do differently?

"Well, I could ask Mr. Whitlock for a referral. He is thrilled with the results he's getting."

"Great idea. Do it. What else could you do?" . . .

This level of interaction with your team members is called managing the gap—a method shown in Figure 2.1.

If the standard is eight calls a week, and Mary is three below it, you have a *gap* of three calls after week one. If you don't act then, the teachable moment is lost. By next week, she might be six behind, and nine the week after that, and so on.

For that very reason, there is no time like the present to act.

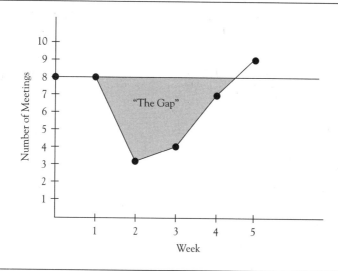

Figure 2.1   Managing the Gap

Shovel the piles when they are small is a good mantra for disciplining your salespeople. It's much easier to make a small course correction than a huge one later.

That's another gem from Steven Brown's book *13 Fatal Errors Managers Make and How to Avoid Them.* One of the greatest things about Brown's book is that just by reading the table of contents, you'll get a great primer on what *not* to do. Imagine if you knew what those fatal errors were in advance—and *didn't* have to make them.

One more important thing about standards: It is better to have a few standards that you enforce than to have dozens of standards that you don't enforce. Because you *will* be tested. I can promise you that.

Sales people will rebel. They will see how far they can push you. They want to know if you're serious about the standards you claim to have set, or are just wishing and hoping that they'll meet them.

Speaking of standards, Matrix Fitness has a beautiful facility outside Madison, Wisconsin. Getting a potential customer to this state-of-the-art health club and to tour headquarters can often seal the deal. But senior VP Kent Stevens has a standard for who he invites to take tours:

> We've [had instances where we've] flown a customer out here to take a look around, [and spent a good amount of time with them and money on them—only to find out later that they hadn't put money down on a location [to even open a club of their own! So], one of our new standards [is that anyone with whom we meet] has to have a lease on a space where they might actually [purchase and] put our equipment.

Another one of my clients was the owner of a Dallas radio station. He set a minimum order standard for his sales team: They were not allowed to bring in an order that was under $5,000 per month. That was the minimum order a sales rep was allowed to sell to an advertiser.

One day a salesperson waltzed into the office with a $4,800 order. The sales manager took it to the owner to see if he could put it on the air.

"No," said the owner.

"But it's only $200 shy."

"Then ask the rep to write a $200 check."

No kidding. That's what happened. The rep had to make up the difference. There was a consequence for not performing up to the standard.

You may think that is an extreme example, or that it's not that big a deal. But here's what happened: Everybody told that story. It became part of the corporate culture. Veterans pulled the new sales reps aside and said, "Never come in here with an order that's less than $5,000." As a result, the reps asked for—and got—bigger orders. Clients bought enough advertising each month to get results in the Dallas market.

When a standard becomes part of the culture, you really have something. You are no longer policing everything; your team is passing on the standards. And that is a big deal.

One of my clients asked a popular local football coach to address his sales meeting and give his team a talk on teamwork and motivation. During the Question and Answer session, one of the salespeople asked the coach how he enforced curfew and kept the players out of the bars.

"I don't. The seniors on our team control the locker room and pass along the rules and culture. If I had to police all of that, I could never do any game planning or run practices."

Think about that answer. Do you have senior sellers who act as surrogate managers to your younger team members?

What would be the value in that?

What stories do you want every salesperson to know and be able to pass along?

As you have probably figured out by now, you influence this with the way you set and enforce standards. A consequence for not making the standard can be a meeting to discuss how to close the gap and make progress toward the standard. Lack of progress toward the standard could ultimately mean dismissal. But smaller consequences come first.

First things first: Find out what is already *actually happening*. Structure and rules work only when they are based in reality. To that end, here are seven questions you need to answer before you set standards:

1. **How many new customers have your salespeople gotten to write checks to your company in the last quarter or last year?** New business development is a critical metric; it is everyone's job to bring in new business. But it is also

very time consuming and takes multiple meetings. *Number of new customers* is one metric that tells you who is selling and who is simply maintaining customers.

2. **What is the average size of an order?** If you require that salespeople bring in new business, they will comply. But you want to go beyond simply having them sell your product or service; you want to deploy them on accounts that will bring in average or above-average sized orders.

3. **How many meetings does it take to land an order?** If it takes multiple meetings, then I suggest you consider every one of those meetings a new business call until the account is writing you checks. Otherwise, you can create a flurry of first meetings on which your salespeople never follow up.

4. **How many accounts does it take to make up 80 percent of your monthly, quarterly, and annual revenue?** This number will give you an instant understanding of how to grow the business—and it reveals another, just-as-important number, which is . . .

5. **How many accounts does it take to make up the last 20 percent of your business?** You will find that the last 20 percent of your business is just as hard to bring in as the first 80 percent—if not harder. If your salespeople are spending 50 percent or more of their time on the last 20 percent of the dollars, they need to see how much easier their jobs would be if they would simply ask for more dollars or spend less time on the smaller accounts and instead focus on potentially larger ones.

6. **How many calls do the top 30 percent make compared to the bottom 30 percent?** You might find they are making more. However, you might also find that they are making fewer calls with much higher quality and that's

why they close more. Crunch the data before you give people assignments that even your best employees couldn't accomplish.

7. **Did you do what you tell your salespeople to do?** What would you want from a manager who wanted this kind of performance out of you?

Every salesperson will claim to be slammed and time-starved. They will declare that they don't have time to do in-depth analyses of their time and efforts, because they are already working impossible hours and working harder than ever. Once they understand how hard they are working for the last 20 percent, they will make much better choices.

Standards and discipline are inextricably linked. Standards that are developed with the team tend to be easier to implement than ones that are dicated from on high.

Hard Lesson #11: You Can Be an Umpire or a Referee. Consequences and You

You have seen that discipline doesn't have to involve chastisement. Still it is difficult for many sales managers—new ones especially to embrace discipline as part of their jobs. Because it is so important, let's look a discipline in a slightly different way.

When you watch a Major League Baseball game, take special notice of what happens when a manager disagrees with an umpire's call. The manager comes out of the dugout and starts to make a case that he already knows he will not win. He may become increasingly demonstrative, violating the umpire's personal space by getting into his face. Sometimes you can even see the manager's saliva spraying on the umpire.

And the umpire takes it. Until . . .

The manager leaves or is pulled back by a coach and a player. Or the umpire throws him out of the game.

You will discover very early in your career that salespeople—much like baseball managers—will test your patience and your tolerance very quickly. You'll also realize that you can't always fire them just because they have gotten under your skin. You have to balance your desire to get rid of someone with the consequences it will have on sales results. While the umpire can throw people out of the game, there is a player on the bench who can carry on; or the bench coach can assume the role of manager for the rest of the game.

If you have a strong bench, you may be able to fire people at will. If that's the case, then go for it. Fire away.

But as a very wise man said, "The firing gun isn't always loaded."

Think about how many players get thrown out of NFL games compared to MLB games, despite the fact that football is a much more aggressive sport. You might assume that football players would be more likely to go off in the heat of what truly is a pitched battle on any given Sunday.

But go watch a National Football League game. Notice what happens when a player gets out of line. The referee throws the flag, and the team is penalized—the *whole* team. If the player gets in the referee's face, there may be another 15-yard penalty. By that time, his teammates are physically dragging the player off the field, and order prevails.

The umpire, in contrast, has to take the player's lip or throw the bum out—while the referee can penalize players 5, 10, and 15 yards. Ejection is always a possibility, but there are less severe consequences that occur before that.

You always want to start out as a referee instead of an umpire. Virtually every manager with whom I spoke in my research for this book admitted that they waited too long to act on a problem. "You assume that the person will pick up the job," said one. "But you really need to jump in and make course corrections more quickly than you do."

Because of that, there are two words with which I want you to become very comfortable, very quickly:

1. Discipline
2. Consequences

You need to think like a referee instead of an umpire—in terms of 5-, 10-, and 15-yard penalties before you even consider ejection or firing.

In order to get comfortable with the word *discipline* you will need to choose the right definition. According to Merriam-Webster's online dictionary, the etymology of *discipline* is from the Latin *disciplina* for teaching, or learning, which stems from *dicipulus* or *pupil*. So while a lot of us hear *discipline* and think *punishment*, a better way to think about discipline is as "training that corrects, molds, or perfects the mental faculties or moral character."

Discipline is a chance to make a small correction in a salesperson's behavior before that behavior intensifies and sinks the salesperson's career. You not only have the right to make these course corrections; it is your duty to do so.

Like I said, most sales managers with whom I have worked over the years have a lot more wishes than they do standards.

I thinking you won't be one of them. Am I right?

"Austin, We Have a Problem"

Make sure you think about the standards you set and how far you are willing to go to enforce them. Standards can have unintended consequences.

A sales manager at an Austin, Texas, radio station attempted to lay down the law to his retail sales team. He had learned that 9 A.M. to 4 P.M. were prime selling hours, so he told the team that nobody was allowed in the building between those hours. They were to be out selling, and should complete their phone and paperwork at their desks only before 9 and after 4.

His top three producers complied—or so he thought. In reality, they had rented a studio apartment a few blocks from their office to set up a satellite office so they could come and go as they pleased.

Clearly, this is not what the manager had intended when he set his parameters. However, he didn't know about the situation until it was way too late. The lesson is to think things through.

You have a goal you want to achieve that is expressed as a dollar figure. And you have standards—measurable indicators of performance—which are how you are going to achieve that goal.

The goal is not to have standards. You have standards so you and your team can achieve the goal.

Hard Lesson #12: You are in the Belief Business

When you take over a sales organization's management, you are forced to deal with people's belief systems. Speaker and author Ken Greenwood has thought long and hard about the plight of the new sales manager.

"Generally speaking, a person is promoted to the position of sales manager because something is wrong. Companies rarely replace a manager when things are running smoothly. Therefore, you have to be in a position of influencing people's thinking to make this transition successfully. And in order to influence your salespeople's beliefs, you have to know what they believe to begin with. Managers make a substantial mistake during sales meetings when they don't take time to listen to a salesperson's story about their success with something they did."

I consider Ken my own personal Peter Drucker. Since he's a well-read and well-traveled executive and a trainer, I called Ken to look at how we get into people's heads and change beliefs. He let me in on some valuable insights. "For starters, within the first 30 days of your tenure, you need to have the following conversation with each member of your sales team. (And if you've been on the job more than 30 days—do it anyway.)

- I want to be able to trust you. How can I know that I am able to trust you? Are you uncomfortable with the idea that someone trusts you? How valuable is trust in your relationships with others?
- What are your needs? What do you need to feel good about yourself?
- I would expect that you to want to continue to learn. Would you consider mentoring someone on staff? (Since the teaching process tends to strengthen one's belief system.)
- I want you to set goals in terms of income. Have you had income goals in the past? What were they?
- What is the quality of your accounts?
- What gives you a feeling of success?
- What can I do to help you at this point in your career?
- How often do you want to get together and review what's going on?

"Giving a salesperson new information is rarely enough to cause that person to change his or her convictions. While you can occasionally influence mindsets, you have to know what people already believe in order to do so," Ken told me.

That last idea is critical. We tell salespeople things. We fill their ears with new information, but it rarely gets to their brains. They don't easily change their convictions or their behavior. To drive that point home, I'm going to give you some new information. And I want you to notice how strongly you resist it. Here goes: We all know that the current obesity crisis our nation is facing is caused by eating too much and exercising too little. That's an indisputable fact.

Or is it?

Gary Taubes is an award-winning science writer who got a $700,000 advance from his publisher to write the definitive book on diet and obesity. *Good Calories, Bad Calories* was published in 2007 after five years of exhaustive research and writing. One of Taubes' conclusions was that obesity is a disease of fat production, not a disease of overeating. In fact, he found that people don't get fat because they overeat; rather, they overeat because they are fat. Turns out that the carbohydrates and low fat foods the "experts" have been telling Americans to eat cause the body to produce insulin. And insulin is the hormone that drives fat production.

Most of us think fat people are undisciplined and lazy. In reality, they are usually doing what their doctors tell them to do, eating less and exercising more.

Unsurprisingly, many people immediately labeled Taubes' conclusion as complete heresy.

In order to accept Gary Taubes' hypothesis, it is necessary to unlearn much of the information we've all come to accept as *true*. For example, you have to reject the idea that you have to burn off more calories than you consume in order to maintain a healthy weight. For me it clicked when Taubes described the fact that we used to call exercise "working up an appetite. Exercise makes you hungry so you eat more.

You would have to give up a long-held belief in order to accept this new information. And that's hard. It's like trying to convince a vegan to join you for dinner at a steakhouse.

Here's what's going on:

New information that doesn't fit with your belief system creates a state called *cognitive dissonance.*

I like the definition from Britannica Online, which defines this as

> . . . the mental conflict that occurs when beliefs or assumptions are contradicted by new information. The unease or tension that the conflict arouses in a person is relieved by one of several defensive maneuvers: the person rejects, explains away, or avoids the new information, persuades himself that no conflict really exists, reconciles the differences, or resorts to any other defensive means of preserving stability or order in his conception of the world and of himself. The concept, first introduced in the 1950s, has become a major point of discussion and research.

Here's how this belief thing applies directly to you and your situation.

Let's say that you have a salesperson covering a territory that should yield $10,000,000 in sales who believes that $500,000 is a lot of money for any single salesperson to bring in. Your job is to get into that person's head in an attempt to change their beliefs about what "a lot of money" is. Or, you have to assign that person to a territory where $500,000 would be a stretch, and let them work to maximize that territory.

This is why it is necessary to ask the questions cited above about income goals, and where they see themselves in the future. The answers will let you know if you are dealing with someone who believes in his ability and wants to accept greater challenges, or just someone who is happy to have a job—no matter what it pays.

You want to get the salesperson's story. And as their coach, you will have to listen to it and confront the beliefs behind it. We all have a story that helps us make sense of the world. Even if it doesn't make sense to others—and even if it isn't true—we all tend to hold on to our own stories. They define and comfort us, even if they don't necessarily help us advance professionally.

In order to learn something new, you have to admit that you didn't know something, were wrong about it, or need new information. This is not an easy thing for adults to do. I'm a big fan of a Phoenix, Arizona-based executive coach named Steve Chandler who tackles this subject in his books and seminars. In his fascinating book *The Story of You*, Chandler quotes Dr. Thomas Szasz, author of *The Myth of Mental Illness* (1974), by citing the fact that "every act of conscious learning requires the willingness to suffer an injury to one's self-esteem. That is why young children learn so easily; they are not yet aware of their own self-importance. It's also why many older persons—especially those who are vain or self-important—cannot learn at all."

As you encourage the learning process in your workplace and make your salespeople responsible for their own development, you will run into resistance and refusal to change. You may wonder why.

Because—as Dr. Thomas Szasz discovered—learning usually hurts.

This is why it is so very crucial to discover the underlying foundation of your salespeople's belief systems. What do they think about themselves and their abilities? What do they want for themselves, and think they deserve? Where are they going and how can you help?

Chances are that you are having one of two reactions right now:

1. Wow, that's a great idea. I need to sit down and really find out what my salespeople are thinking.
2. Wow, that's *way* too much work. I'd rather show and tell them what to do, because that's what my boss did for me.

If you resist the notion that truly effective sales management means working with and on your salespeople's beliefs, then you're simply feeling the pain of the assault on your own self esteem. The fact that you feel it—and resist it—will allow you feel exactly how your salespeople do when they are attempting to process new information that challenges their beliefs or contradicts their stories.

Hard Lesson #13: Your Top Producer May Not Be Your Top Performer and Customers Buy In Spite of Salespeople

There are plenty of wonderful people in sales. There are very few great salespeople, though. M&T Bank's Lowell Yoder calls them the *five percenters*, and describes them as follows: "A five percenter is someone who has all the innate skills and talents to be a top performer without the help of training, coaching, and mentoring. The remaining 95 percent of us can benefit from a sales process and methodology that we can follow that increases our chance of success," says Yoder.

Whether it's 5 percent or the 20 percent of the salespeople who, if Pareto is to be believed, make 80 percent of the sales, the majority of salespeople are what speaker and author Don Beveridge calls *professional visitors*, or what I call *Level 1 Salespeople*. Their call objective is to see what's happening instead of trying to make something happen, and their pre-meeting preparation is to make sure they have the latest marketing materials and price sheets in their briefcases. They're product-focused rather than customer and problem focused.

Part of the sales manager's balancing act is to get people in front of the right prospects and customers with the right message. Salespeople who lead with price sheets and product literature duplicate the efforts of your web site. If a customer really wanted your prices and literature, they would have already downloaded the PDF that's on your web site.

Sales people who add value get longer meetings and more referrals.

What most customers want from salespeople is an understanding of their problems and some information that they don't know already.

Cliff Albert, director of sales at Berry Plastics, is a proponent of this kind of information-led sales approach:

> In our business, there's a true lack of knowledge about where your products end up. We have to get past the distributor and connect with the end user. If Marketing understood [that] a single mother of two typically buys plastic plates at a party store to use on a day to day basis so she doesn't have to do dishes, that information could help us target our sales and marketing efforts better demographically. Where should we go? Instead of calling on the food service distributor, we might

want to call on the party store distributor. That's the level of information that a salesperson doesn't extract from a buyer at a corporate buying house. That [knowledge] makes us even more valuable to our distributor, because now I can take marketing into a customer.

This is what we see from a macro level; this is where you should channel some of your energy, because this is where we see the business. Then we become a little bit more valuable.

In my world, I am selling to distributors like Sysco and United Food Systems. And my division [is] selling to institutions: school systems, hospitals, catering companies. But those institutions also have a customer. So I am three customers removed from the end user—and most of those people in the middle aren't sophisticated enough to know what the end user really wants. Therefore, if we are able to communicate this information back to Sysco or United Food Service buyers, they are willing listeners. They really want people to tell them where they should be focusing their business. It's powerful stuff.

The buyers at the distributor level just want to move cases. They don't spend—or have—the time to find out where these cases are going. So when you come in and say, "Look, we are seeing caterers moving in the direction of plastic products that are very similar to ceramics"—then they listen. And the buyer will say something like, "Have you told my salespeople this? You've got to sit with them." The minute the buyer lets you talk about the business a little bit and recognizes that you know something about it, they understand that you are there as a supplier to help her build her company. When you can get that hook, you move away from being a commodity supplier to an [actual] resource.

It's not easy, but it all starts with data. Everybody wants your data. We use a service called Technomics that reports on the food service business. Everybody wants to see our report. They don't want to pay for it, but they want to see it.

Tim McMahon, now at Creighton University describes the new kind of relationship that salespeople have with today's buyer at Walmart. McMahon made the trip to Bentonville Arkansas when he was with a Fortune 100 firm that sold to the giant retailer:

> We talk about relationships in sales. A CEO might say to a VP of Sales, "I thought you had a good relationship with those guys. How come you can't get us in there?" Well, what is a relationship, [really]? When you go to Bentonville to sell Walmart, there is a buying office with identical cubes that are glass from the waist up. The buyer walks into the cube, and you have 45 or 50 minutes to make your sale. You can't look at the credenza behind the buyer and say, "Oh, I see Tommy plays football." They erase small talk like that; they've likely only been on the account for six months or less. Walmart actually rotates the buyers constantly because they don't *want* relationships to form. Having a relationship with a buyer [today] has nothing to do with things like knowing [their wives or kids' names], [chatting about their hobbies, or becoming] good buddies. The relationship that's valuable is the one [wherein someone knows] their buyers' business—one where he can say, "I know what you need. I don't have to waste time asking you stupid questions. We can get to the heart of the matter, to the problems and implications and payoffs." That's the kind of relationship the buyer wants. And actually it's the kind of relationship the seller wants, too.

Bringing information to the table about your customers' customer adds value to every meeting your salespeople have with prospects and customers. But the norm is that salespeople present products and pricing, and then field price objections.

My colleague for two decades, Mark Peterson is a nationally known expert in psychometric testing who helps companies hire salespeople who can operate in demanding environments. He describes the problem amiable salespeople face in this kind of environment.

> Salespeople who have a need to be liked have trouble with this kind of reality. They are not going to find a lot of friends in the field. But truly great salespeople don't need to be liked. They aren't your enemy; but they don't necessarily want to be your best friend, either. When you need the client's approval, you stop yourself short of asking tough questions—even to the point of not asking for the sale, because someone might be offended.

Monitoring salespeople's pre-meeting plans, bringing buyers into your sales meetings, evaluating the quality of your sales calls and yes, having standards for what a good meeting and high performance look like is part of your job description.

Hard Lesson #14: Salespeople Often Do Their Best Selling in Your Office

Maybe you can identify with the following frustrated CEO (who didn't want me to use his name). His company had a brand new sales initiative they were ready to roll out. When he visited one of his business units, he heard price objections—from his own sales team.

> What I learned right off the bat is that we negotiate prices inside [the] building before we even go out the door with the new offering. The salespeople had already determined among themselves that the new offering was overpriced. No one had

even presented it to a customer and gotten price resistance. They decided internally as a sales team that the market couldn't bear it.

Salespeople learn very early in their careers that their prices are too high. But instead of being proud of the high price and superior quality, they start agreeing with their customers and trying to convince management to lower the prices to save the business.

Another important responsibility you have as sales manager is to instill pride in higher prices, sell value, and hold margins. This is easier said than done for publicly traded companies who are trying to make a number they promised Wall Street. It is why companies constantly go to the well with the low-cost special deal as the quarter comes to a close. This then becomes a self-perpetuating tactic because your salespeople train your customers to wait until the price comes down.

Let me give you two examples from my own life that I hope you will be able to apply to your unique situation. Most agencies in the advertising business will tell you what to charge for your commercials based on your ratings. You either take the amount they want to pay, or walk away from the deal. Unless, of course, there is so much demand on your inventory that you can walk away from a low margin deal; otherwise, you may be forced to take it.

A conversation regarding this scenario might go something like this:

Potential advertiser: "Your rates are too high."

Our salesperson: "I understand. At the same time, there is so much pressure on our inventory that I'm unable to offer you a lower rate. We only have eight minutes of commercials per hour and there are 11 other salespeople out there right now trying to sell them to your competitors so they can get our listeners to shop at their store instead of yours. Let's focus on the value of getting this commercial heard by another 15,000 of our listeners. What is your average sale? And what is the lifetime value of a customer?"

Now, let's break down that answer into four steps.

1. The **panic-button** answer to any objection is, "I understand. And at the same time . . ."
2. Sell **scarcity**. Let them know that there is not an unlimited supply of this product.
3. Shift the focus to the **prospect's need** to sell his product or solve her problem.
4. Focus on making the things listed in number 3 **happen**.

I have run many sales meetings with the purpose of having attendees memorize an answer to the price objection. We write it down on a 3×5 index card and have each person around the table read it aloud. Then, we ask one person to say the first sentence from memory. The person to the first person's right says the second sentence, and so on. Then we ask one person to recite the entire statement from memory until he can't go on with the rest of the people looking at the card to help him—much like the person on stage who feeds actors their forgotten lines. Then the next person tries it from memory with coaching. Within 15 minutes, everyone has memorized the answer. Though you might have to practice it again in a few weeks because people have forgotten, this is the way you get people to sell their customers instead of their managers.

When I was on the road 225 days a year, conducting 130 seminars, we had our first seller who billed a half million dollars a year. Carol Joy Green sold our seminars and distance-learning programs. Whenever someone asked if she could give them a better deal, she would pause for a few beats and then say these words like she had just thought of them: "I understand you have to ask that question. At the same time, why would you buy sales training designed to get your people go get higher prices from a company that immediately caves on its price? Chris's calendar is already filled and there are only three open dates this quarter. Do you want to lock one in?"

You get the idea.

If you don't prepare your salespeople to justify and get a higher margin sale from the customer, you should be prepared to spend hours negotiating with them to get a lower price, so that they can *earn* the client's business.

Another issue—especially with young salespeople—is that they tend to think that whatever they make in salary or commission is a lot of money. When you make $36,000 a year, asking a customer to spend $3,000 a month is daunting. It is up to you to read their proposals before they give them to customers. You are the one who will set standards for them for minimum *asks* and minimum billable orders. I was fortunate enough early in my career to have a trainer tell me that I had to start asking for a lot more money from my customers than I I was making in salary and commissions.

Your job is to explain that there is a difference between *business* and *personal* dollars. Before eTickets, there were days when I left my office with $5,000 worth of airline tickets in the inside pocket of my suit. I rarely thought much about it. Upon returning home, I might go to an art fair or gallery and see a painting that cost $5,000. "Wow, that's a lot of money," I would think. See, business dollars and personal dollars are two completely different things.

Let's go back to that $36,000 a year salesperson. There is a car dealership in Madison, Wisconsin, that has multiple locations. Their coffee budget is $36,000 a month! Business dollars and personal dollars are two different things.

So, how will you get your salespeople to be braver about asking for more money? What stories can you tell them about how you learned to ask for and get bigger and bigger orders before you got promoted?

Power, Clout, and You

"Do you see what it says on my business card? Right here, under my name, it says *Sales Manager*. Get out your card and read what it says underneath your name. Never mind, I'll tell you what it says. It says *Account Manager*. I manage you. You manage the accounts. Now do what I say."

When you become the sales manager, you get the title, but you don't get nearly as much power as you think you have.

I recall reading an article about sales force compensation in the *Harvard Business Review*. The gist of the article was that if salespeople earn 70 percent or more of their income in commission, they feel like they work for themselves. It is much harder for a manager to influence their behavior when the commission has so much of their attention. Salespeople who earn 70 percent of their income through salary and can earn 30 percent or more in incentives for accomplishing objectives tend to be influenced by company policy and sales manager's directions. Objectives include making quota, pursuing new business, retaining customers, selling the complete line, and so on.

What gets rewarded gets done. When 30 percent of your income is tied to an MBO like new business development or customer retention, then salespeople prospect and service their customers. Most Fortune 500 companies have a compensation plan that drives behavior.

Many start-ups; small businesses; and high turnover, sales-person-churning companies pay a non-living wage. Essentially, they want salespeople to work as hard as they can to make as much as they can.

As the sales manager, the less your company compensates people up front, the less clout you have with them. They believe they work for themselves. And basically, they do.

Realtors are a great example. They are independent contractors and the owner of the real estate office provides them with a desk and a phone (in some cases) and lets them loose on the community to get listings and sell houses.

No matter how often you have wanted to say to a salesperson what I said in the first paragraph of this section, flaunting your position power rarely works.

You have the most *clout*—position-power wise—with brand new hires who are still trying to impress you and who are still on probation. You can lay down the law and require compliance. The veterans are an entirely different case.

Most compensation programs make it impossible to be the boss and imperative to be the leader. What's the difference? Leaders use a blend of position power and personal power to drive behavior.

Let's say that your boss and her bosses or the board have been meeting to rework the compensation plan. The stockholders have spoken. They've hired the compensation consultant and she has given them the new plan, which they hand to you to hand to the sales force.

You are the one who is going to have to manage the fallout at the level where the salespeople perceive that their entitlement to a six-figure salary has just been yanked.

Because leadership style is infectious in organizations, barking CEOs beget barking VPs and barking VPs beget barking regional managers and so on down the line.

Your job as the leader is to use your personal power as well as your position power to *get buy-in* for the new compensation plan. That may mean meeting one of your top salespeople for dinner and saying something like, "I need your support. Our board is looking to control costs, and next year's compensation plan, while fair, looks to create increased activities and reward higher margins. I'm not asking you to like it. I'm just asking you to be supportive in the sales meeting where I have to sell it. Will you help me with this? I'll remember it if you do."

You can reward the salesperson as you see fit. You can give them an extra lead or look the other way when they knock off early on a summer afternoon. But you need allies and people who take your side at the meeting *after* the sales meeting at the coffee shop around the corner.

The more senior and experienced a worker is, the more you can offer support. Novices require more direction from you. "Dial the phone." "Go to the networking events." "Take a client to one of these three restaurants." As people become more experienced and capable, you can show interest and offer some coaching. However, in saying things like, "I trust you to do the right thing," and, "It's your customer. You make that call," you are offering support.

The "A" Word and You

Holding people accountable is something great sales managers do. You have to develop salespeople who are willing to accept responsibility for what they do—and what they've done. When I asked Phil Fisher about his philosophy of sales management, he told me, "The idea [is that] you want to make salespeople accountable." Before customer relationship management (CRM) systems appeared on the scene, Fisher devised a system of *white sheets* for each account the salesperson was calling on. "You had all the trappings of how they organized and ran the accounts—including how much the order was and how much they projected, and how far they were into the account. This gave me the opportunity to review the accounts at all times." Fisher looked at activity on every account every week.

Today's CRM programs are only as good as the data salespeople enter into them. The first time you don't get a call report or an update in the CRM system is the first time you should place the call to the delinquent salesperson. You cannot coach or influence them unless you know what is happening.

You want optimizers, people who will figure out on their own how to make their goals and work their territory. But if you don't have those, you need to give them systems so they can work with the structure you create.

Are You Managing for Compliance or Leading for Commitment?

My late colleague Norm Goldsmith was a partner of mine in The Leadership Institute. He wondered if you could create some precision language around commitment and compliance. His chart (Figure 2.2) is a page taken out of the workbook that our participants used. Norm would ask each manager to read the description and then on the right, pencil in the names of the people on his team who most closely fit the definition.

You might want to do the same thing. But make a photocopy first. I'll tell you why after you complete the exercise.

Level of Commitment	Name of Person

COMMITMENT
Will make it happen. Creates the structure needed. Owns it. Accountable. No
excuses!

_____
_____
_____
_____
_____

RESPONSIBILITY
Needs it to happen. Is conscientious. Will
go the extra mile within the "spirit of the
law," but if the situation is beyond their
control, well. . . .

_____
_____
_____
_____
_____

GENUINE COMPLIANCE
Wants it to happen. Good soldier. Follows
the "letter of the law." But if that's not
good enough, it's not their fault. Think
they are doing the best they can.

_____
_____
_____
_____
_____

GRUDGING COMPLIANCE
Would like it to happen. Will go along if
it's no extra trouble. Won't volunteer
extra effort. Has a "What can you
expect?" attitude.

_____
_____
_____
_____
_____

NONCOMPLIANCE
Hopes it happens but not that much.
Either think they can't or won't be fired,
or "It's no big deal" if they are.

_____
_____
_____
_____
_____

Observations from this analysis:

_____
_____
_____
_____

**Figure 2.2 Assessing the Levels of Commitment of Your
Key People**

Where do your salespeople fall on this scale? Do you have several names beside COMMITMENT, or only one or two? How far down the scale do your people go? It is true that there are times when COMPLIANCE is acceptable. Not everybody can be committed to every initiative and every demand placed upon them. But are you tolerating anyone who is too low on the scale for your comfort or the good of the company? How many people can you move from GRUDGING COMPLIANCE to GENUINE COMPLIANCE?

The reason I instructed you to make a copy for your own use is that I want you to make a copy for every member of your sales team. Send it to them or drop it on their desks. Ask them to look over the words and the definitions. Schedule meetings with them so that they can tell you where they rated themselves and why. Use that meeting as an opportunity to share with the person where you put them on this continuum, and why. This will enable you to have a civil conversation about what you would like from that person, and the salesperson will tell you where they want to be on the continuum.

Do you see how this might be a useful tool in a one-on-one meeting? When will you hold that meeting? What's the worst—and the best—that could happen as a result?

Stage 3 Tasks

Developing the People Who Develop Your Profits and Put Out Their Own Fires

B usiness writer Julia Chang interviewed me for an article for *Sales and Marketing Management* magazine. Her very first questions were, "What do you think separates the A players from the B players in sales? Conversely, what are some of the roadblocks that often keep B players from becoming A players?" Here is what I told her:

> A players orchestrate the sale. B players accommodate the buyer.

That seemingly simple answer, however, has profound implications. Do your salespeople orchestrate—"arrange or combine so as to achieve a desired or maximum effect"—or do they accommodate, meaning they are agreeable to customers, but do not stand up for themselves?

The week of the interview, Sarah McCann—my partner and wife— was orchestrating a twentieth anniversary bash for Cindi Gerber, our company's first employee. On Saturday morning, I called Sarah from the Phoenix airport. She was already preparing food for the Sunday evening dinner for 50 people. She had scheduled kitchen help to be there at 9:00 A.M. and 1:00 P.M. She had booked the DJ and lined up the limo.

Why am I telling this story? Because A players orchestrate a sale much like Sarah orchestrates a dinner party. They start with the image of the event they want to create (confirming the order) and arrange the steps they'll need to take to create that event. They rely on a repeatable formula that they use with every customer. They don't have to reinvent their sales process for every single buyer.

Entertainment Weekly once profiled Las Vegas legend Wayne Newton. The reporter went to every show for two weeks and was able to break down Newton's formula. There is the *walk of kisses*, the salute to the veterans in the audience, and the *song we didn't rehearse*. It's the same show night after night. That shouldn't come as a shock. Pros follow a process that works over and over again. Pilots go through a preflight checklist for every takeoff. My doctor gives me the same physical every year. Sarah has a formula for putting on a dinner party. The neighborhood Christmas party had a different menu than Cindi's party—but her basic formula does not vary. All of these people have found success in doing these things a particular way; they aren't going to change their methods.

Here's the secret that A players know and B players refuse to accept: The steps they take, the questions they ask, the things they ask for, and the order in which they do these things are the same—time after time. The people change, but the formula holds fast. What keeps this from becoming boring is that it *works*—and it works because A players know exactly what they are going to do and why. This allows them to completely focus on the particular person they are going to do it with. That's where the real variety in selling occurs—and even that variety is relatively slight. All businesses have problems—most of which are universal and not unique to a particular company. Still, there are nuances that make the listening interesting.

The Mysterious Mindset of the B Player

For reasons that cannot be understood, B players believe that each sale is a brand new, uncharted undertaking. Though they may have heard of a sales process, they haven't internalized one. Maybe they don't trust theirs—or themselves—enough to follow it. But as soon as the buyer objects to something or offers an alternate plan, the B player cannot oblige quickly enough.

Here's an example of how B players accommodate the buyer: Let's say that the first meeting in their sales process requires them to do a demonstration in order to sufficiently impress the prospect with their solution. They want the prospect to engage with them after the demo, which takes 25 minutes from start to finish, since their offering requires considerable explanation.

After the 25-minute demo, the salesperson knows that it's going to take at least 35 more minutes for the customer to ask questions, provide information, and let them suggest the next step. Therefore, they need an hour—but the buyer will only give them 15 minutes. So, they immediately take the 15 minutes and cut and paste their demonstration to accommodate the prospect.

They don't try to sell the prospect on their process and why they need the time they're asking for. B players allow the customer to dictate all the terms—putting themselves at an immediate disadvantage for the rest of the relationship. They don't assert themselves up front and sell the need for a longer meeting. They don't think, "Hey, wait a minute! I'm going to drive 60 miles to see this prospect, and 60 miles home. I'm investing most of my day to meet with her."

They don't assert themselves by saying something like this: "With the price of sales calls at an all-time high, wouldn't you want *your* salespeople to negotiate a longer meeting before they got in the car or hopped on a plane to see a potential customer?" That's what an A player would say. But B players accommodate the buyer. They take the 15 minutes, rush through the demo or ignore it all together, make a fairly weak impression, and—this is what really kills me—they thank the buyer for *her* time at the end of the meeting when they have invested a day, and the buyer has only invested 15 minutes.

The Seven Roadblocks

The following are the seven major roadblocks that most often keep B players from becoming A players:

Roadblock 1: B players don't have a philosophy of selling. They haven't developed the belief that their time is as valuable as their customer's time. They don't know that they add value by making the call. They haven't been taught about selling or received enough coaching from their boss to develop that philosophy. "The unexamined life is not worth living," said Socrates. To which I would add, "The unexamined sales call is not worth making." Thinking about what you do is a critical part of the sales job and getting salespeople to *think* is a critical part of yours.

Roadblock 2: Having a manager who doesn't hold a salesperson accountable to a process that works. This is a rampant problem.

Roadblock 3: Fear of (1) looking scripted, (2) not doing it perfectly, (3) appearing pushy, and (4) of success.

Roadblock 4: Not asking for clarification from a manager or an A player, but hanging out with other B players and commiserating about how tough things are in the field.

Roadblock 5: Lack of repetition and practice. B players seem to be willing to stay where they are, and are content to be *good enough*—as long as they don't get fired.

Roadblock 6: B players are focused on their own insecurity, income, and problems. They don't realize that their prospect is just as insecure and probably has at least as many problems as they do. Instead, they reason that they have a problem, and the customer has the money. A players understand that they have a solution to a problem that is costing the customer lots of money.

Roadblock 7: B players worry about being liked instead of being of service.

To accommodate or to orchestrate? That is the question. There is only one answer.

You need A players on your sales team. You can develop them, steal them from the competition, or recruit them. The free agent syndrome is alive and well. We make industry experience the number one hiring criteria. "Big mistake," according to the Performance Group's Jim Lobaito. Here's why:

> It's the most overrated criteria and most sales managers are blinded by that one characteristic. What you are really saying when you say, "I need someone with industry experience" is "We really don't have a good onboarding and orientation program. So we need to find someone with industry relationships so that they can hopefully carry over."
>
> Well, relationships don't carry over anymore because companies will tolerate bad performance from a current supplier so they don't have to make another change. Customers won't follow a salesperson like they did 10 or 15 years ago.

Hiring expert, Mark Peterson's (www.petersonandassociates .com) take is that we look for people with industry experience because that's the criteria on which outside recruiters focus. But just because someone has industry experience doesn't mean they can sell. If you test these salespeople before you hire them, you will find that industry experience does not translate to sales prowess.

So, maybe you need to do some recruiting.

Recruiting A Players: The *Secret* of Being a Great Sales Manager

It is impossible to accomplish big goals without big talent.

Over the course of the decades I've spent as a seminar leader, I was a very frequent flyer. One of the things I used to do to amuse myself was to make lists of all the celebrities I had seen on airplanes and in airports. Like the night in Nashville, Tennessee, when I saw Captain Kangaroo and Jesse Jackson at baggage claim. Or the day at O'Hare when George Burns passed me in a cart with lights flashing and beeper beeping. There have been minor and major rock stars, business moguls, senators, congressmen, TV anchors, and athletes—even entire professional and college teams. But the most frequent flying celebrities I encountered by far have been college coaches on recruiting trips:

- The late Hall of Famer Al McGuire
- Bob Knight
- Denny Crum
- The late Wisconsin football coach Dave McClain
- Hall of Fame coach Lou Holtz
- And many more . . .

What's the lesson for you? These coaches won a lot of games and National Championships because they were relentless recruiters. When you recruit talented people, you leverage every single minute on the practice field. And of course, this applies to you.

You cannot be a hall of fame coach without having blue chip players. Nor can you be a great sales manager without talented salespeople.

Avoid The *Warm Body* Syndrome

Whenever a sales manager says, "I just need a body to fill that position," you can bet he is operating in Stages 1 and 2 of the Sales Management Trap. Not having a ready well of candidates to choose from means you are shirking your duties as sales manager.

Job #1 of sales management is recruitment. Hiring expert Robert Half calls it "incoming quality control." If you're in a big company, you may think that this is HR's job. If you don't make it yours, your department will be as dynamic and entrepreneurial as HR. You don't want that.

You may have noticed the ideal candidate rarely shows up in your lobby when you have an opening. Recruiting and evaluating candidates on an ongoing basis is crucial. "Get ahead of your needs," is how sales management author Jack Falvey puts it.

Set aside time every week—at least every month—to evaluate prospective salespeople. You are going to have an opening someday. Planned or unplanned turnover is part of the process. It is better to have a database full of good candidates to bring back rather than cranking up the recruiting process once you have a need to hire someone.

You want to go fishing in a deep pool, not a shallow puddle. Here's how to start stocking that pool.

It is August 1973, and I am living with my new bride in Newark, Ohio, and working for the radio station in town. I am reading *Broadcasting* magazine and I see a classified ad that I remember to this day.

"**Madison, Wisconsin**: Young, aggressive, problem-solving salesperson to sell top-rated station in the market. If you're good and want a place to grow and advance, send your resume to P.O. Box 2058, etc._____."

We had just moved in to a new apartment, but one of my wife's goals was to get a master's degree in speech pathology. One of the three schools on her list was the University of Wisconsin. So I showed her the ad and said, "I think I should apply for this job so you can go to school and I can get in a bigger market."

"But we just moved into this place," she replied.

"Honey," I said, "we will never have less to move than we do now, and besides, this ad may never run again." (Hold that thought.)

I sent my resume, a picture, and some commercials I had produced. Back then, you could send pictures.

I got the job, mainly because the radio station had a basketball team and I was an athlete, and because I was the only salesperson who had ever submitted a cassette tape with his resume, where the packet went straight to the program director, who was also the team's coach. When he saw I was six feet, three inches tall and had high jumped six feet, eight inches in college, he went to the sales manager and told him that he had better hire me.

The sales manager called me and flew both of us to Madison, took us to dinner, and told us how great it would be to work there. He never really asked me any tough questions. He just went into sales mode.

Two years later, I was the sales manager. You've read that story at the beginning of the book. But here's what I discovered when I moved into the sales manager's office. The classified ad that I had read in bed had been running every week for years and continued to run for many more. There were boxes of resumes to go through and more came every week. It was a 52-week recruitment campaign.

And each week, I would go through the newest resumes and target one or two possibilities to interview. I set a goal to interview at least one person a week whether I needed to or not. I would always make it a point to tell that person that I was interested in talent.

The story is important to you, because the worst time to start recruiting is when you have an opening. And here is my strong recommendation: Use at least seven different recruiting sources besides HR and headhunters. You want to develop your sources of names, applications, and resumes. Here are a few to consider:

- College professors can send you bright young students for interviews and internships. If you hire entry-level salespeople, this is a great source of names. Establish a relationship with a business professor at a local college or community college. Once or twice a year, volunteer to address the professor's class about your industry or sales as a career.

  Phil Fisher has recruited and hired some of broadcasting's great sales talent. He worked a connection at Southern Illinois University.

  When we first started out, 99.5 percent of salespeople on the street for radio stations were male. I got Nancy Martin out of Southern Illinois University. I ran an ad. She answered the ad. And I hired her, which was very unusual. I trained her. She became a very good source of candidates for me. So I kept going back to Southern Illinois University. They had their own radio station and went out and sold advertising. And I got to know Professor Bill Kurtz, who was a terrific guy. Then, I started going down there every year for at least 20 years and recruited the best talent in broadcasting. They were head and shoulders above everyone else in the industry.

I would go down there for two days. On the first day, I would lecture and give them an assignment that they would turn in to their professor. I got to be known as the place you want to go to if you want to start your career in broadcasting.

- Post on job boards, of course, but know that the great salespeople and connected sellers get hired faster than they can post their online profiles.

- Monster.com may be the most famous place to post. Mark Peterson, who consults with clients on recruiting and hiring issues offers this advice:

> I have a client who has been recruiting in Chicago for salespeople—and they have found Craigslist to be the place to go. There's a trick to writing a good recruitment ad: it has to make the job look like something the person would want to do for a living. My client is in the third party medical examination business; they call on insurance companies, risk management departments at large companies, and attorneys who are fighting bogus workman's comp claims. The guys who sell the service spend their days at breakfasts, lunches, dinners, and cocktail parties with their current and prospective customers. We didn't sell them a job [by telling them] what service they'd be selling; we did it by telling them what they were going to be doing. [We let them know that their responsibility was to wine and dine] doctors, lawyers, and executives. We sell the activity in which our salespeople are going to be engaged to attract someone who likes that kind of activity.

- Peterson advises his clients never to advertise the job in terms of how much a salesperson can earn:

We never talk about that. Instead, we advertise that a candidate must have verifiable proof of previous earnings of [whatever the amount is] annually. They need to prove to you that they're worth the kind of money you're expecting them to earn. If they can't prove they've earned 80 percent of that amount, they are probably not a good candidate. We quickly screen out the people who have no business applying for the position, [because this type of ad tends to attract] heavy hitters. I have a client in North Carolina who is looking for salespeople who can make $175,000 a year. They have a big number they require salespeople to have earned previously. And now they have the best team they have ever had after one year of using that strategy and my assessment tools to screen out candidates who are not going to cut it.

- Radio ads that feature your current team telling the listener what *they* like about selling for you will help you reach people who are currently employed and not actively searching for a job.
- Classified newspaper ads are a traditional source
- Job fairs draw crowds of unemployed people, but you may find a gem.
- Company open houses get job seekers on your turf and, held after work, can attract currently employed people to check out your company.
- Company web sites are an obvious place to post your current sales openings.
- Paying Referral fees to your own sales team can get them beating the bushes for talent.
- Your customers can be great recruitment sources. Ask a buyer or an executive who meets with sales reps to name

the top three salespeople she has met with in the past six months. Get as much contact information as you can get. Call the sales rep and say, "I have been asking buyers who are some of the best salespeople they deal with and your name came up. I wanted to let you know that." Because this person's manager may not have recognized him in the last six months, you may catch this person at a vulnerable moment. Just say, "I'm always looking to meet top salespeople to see if they would be interested in selling _____ and whether I can help them achieve their financial and other goals."

- Getting on the phone and talking to a lot of people might work for you. A New York Life area manager once got my name from a friend and called to ask me to go to lunch. At lunch, he asked me for names of the best salespeople I know. I wouldn't reveal the names of my clients, so he asked me who was the best clothing salesperson I'd ever met. Where did I buy my cars? Who sold me my house? Who's the best manager I know? You can bet his next step was to call some of those people and get more names until he had collected resumes and booked interviews. You could do a lot worse than follow that successful model.

- Other sales managers can be a great source of leads. If you have 20 resumes but only one opening, you might consider sharing names with a fellow sales manager in a noncompetitive industry. He could reciprocate to give you more people to interview.

   The Performance Group's Jim Lobaito puts it this way:

> The sales management job is to be actively recruiting. Currently there are three people who I keep in touch with. Because one of these days I will match them to the

right opportunity. One of these relationships is now three years old. But that's what you have to do because top performers aren't on the job market very long. They are on it for two or three days. They don't appear on job boards. They know what their next move is. People know about them. If you are not on their short list, you won't get the call when they are ready to move.

Phil Fisher talked about the importance of hiring people who are both good—and who know it. "The worst guy you can find is the guy who can't grow number one, and number two is not quite bad enough to fire. I was more interested in finding people with potential rather than just rocking along with someone."

Hiring A Players Means Selecting for Traits and Training for Skills

Have you ever hired a salesperson who performed better during the interview process than he did on the job?

You have? I thought so.

Consider testing them and not relying solely on resume reading and interviewing. A personality profile or other validated instrument can give you insight into a candidate's drives, ability to learn, work on commission, and handle adversity.

If you are not using some kind of psychometric instrument to analyze your candidates' intelligence and personality, you will fail many more times than you succeed. An article in *Sales and Management* magazine, "Validation: What the Numbers Show," rates the interview at 14 percent validity, reference checks at 26 percent, biographics (items like the application and resume) at 37 percent, job tryout at 44 percent—and psychometric testing at 53 percent. If you take the approach of assuming (or hoping) that they're going to somehow *become* good after you interview them—and they turn out not to be—then you clearly lack a valid hiring process. You must get a lot of different looks at the candidate from a variety of sources.

Even multiple interviews will not reveal as much information as testing. Mark Peterson is a successful sales professional and his firm sells thousands of assessments to firms all over the country. I asked him the traits we need to find before we hire a salesperson:

I have not yet created a model of a successful salesperson where that person didn't have at least an average to above average level of intelligence. [In other words], you've got to be smart. The second thing that goes right along with this is . . . an innate curiosity. [Good salespeople inherently] want to know things. We can measure that with memory recall of current events and common knowledge, because the people with the best memory recall have a broad range of knowledge. They are aware. They have observation skills and an extensive attention span. They will take [the curiosity they have] and try to understand someone's business situation. Now you become a problem solver as opposed to a salesperson who is just trying to sell something for your reasons, not the prospect's reasons.

Peterson continues,

They also have to have a desire for financial success. It's not just that they want to make a lot of money. The (Dave) Kurlan instrument that I use with my customers tests for desire—and not having it is a knockout factor. If the candidate doesn't desire financial success, they are not considered an attractive candidate. It is this intangible that drives them to do whatever it takes—ethically and legally—to succeed in sales. Desire and commitment are two key issues and on my test you have to pass on both of them.

A couple of other things that are knockout factors for which you can test:

1. Are they **trainable**? Twenty-two percent of salespeople are not. They simply lack the desire to improve—and no one can force them to do so.

2. Forty-one percent of salespeople are **resistant to coaching**. Their own assessment of their talents reveals their impression that they have greater talents than we can validate. They think they know how to prospect . . . or how to handle a first meeting. But when you evaluate the strategies they are using against what is proven not to work, they are in trouble. If they don't have the skills and they are not coachable, then [forget them].

There is a simple way to become a much better judge of sales talent. Peterson works with Profile and Achiever instruments, which measure one's disposition to be a salesperson. Both instruments measure six mental aptitudes and 10 personality dimensions, and connect the dots between the two. He explains,

My favorite instrument is the Dave Kurlan Sales Force Profile (technically called the OMG express screen), which is used for hiring. It gets at what are my sales motivations and whether I have the desire, and commitment. It reveals whether I accept responsibility and have a good outlook. It also gets at specific weaknesses that can neutralize the innate characteristics about wanting to be successful in sales. For instance, if people buy slowly, they sell slowly.

Until a few years ago, we had a division that sold some of these testing services. I have been tested and can tell you it's like standing in front of a mirror naked. Tests reveal more about a candidates more quickly than they would ever reveal in an interview or several interviews.

The Interview, You, and Weeding Out B Players

Testing notwithstanding, you will meet with candidates and interview them, of course. And there are things that will make your interview more reliable and a bit more valid. First, have a prepared list of five must-have characteristics and traits. Then, prepare a list of 10 more traits that you would *like* to have.

Prepare a list of questions that you will ask that will extend the interview to at least 90 minutes. Most candidates can keep up a facade for 45 minutes to an hour. They wear down after that and reveal more of themselves.

And keep reminding yourself that your job is to select instead of settle. Too often, accidental sales managers have a tendency to *sell the job* instead of select a person who can do it well. And there is a big difference between the two.

You can never be a great sales manager until you are leading a group of talented achievers.

Ed Fratz is a former Verizon Sales Director who now specializes in training salespeople in the telecom space. He believes that the human resource department has taken over too much of the recruitment and hiring process. See if you can identify with his reasoning:

HR has a set of questions they ask everyone. The candidate can buy a book on how to answer every one of HR's questions. And HR passes them to the sales manager.

But I want to know how they were brought up and about their work ethic. So one of the questions I ask is, "Tell me about the very first job you ever had and how old you were?"

That's a high yield question. It gets at a person's beliefs and behaviors.

One of the best reps I ever hired told me he was 12 years old when both of his parents lost their jobs so he went down to the harbor and unloaded fish trucks for three hours after school. He did this until he was 18 years old.

I have had a candidate answer that question by saying, "Well, my dad paid for college so this will be my first job." Didn't they babysit, cut lawns—anything? I want to know that they really value working. Having a desire to work hard is important for salespeople.

Another question I asked was, "Tell me what you did to prepare for this interview." I've had three really good answers.

One candidate said, "I Googled you and found out all associations you belong to and the companies you have worked for."

Another person said, "Mr. Fratz, when I met you by phone yesterday, I didn't own a suit. When you said you would interview me I went out and bought a suit." He couldn't afford a suit, but he got one anyway. He demonstrated that he had a whatever-it-takes mentality—and that rep made $90,000 his first year as a retail rep in Huntsville.

Another candidate told me he had memorized every rate plan we had published—and we had 35 rate plans.

But there was one person who said, "I read everything about your company on the web site." So I asked, "What's the name of our CEO?"

"I don't know," said the candidate. So I said, "Do you have any other questions for me?"

Fratz is looking for what drives people to succeed, for the willingness to do what it takes. Garfield Ogilvie, VP of sales for Clear Channel Outdoor, talked to me about the pitfalls of hiring the wrong person and how he probes for real talent and desire. "The hiring piece is so critical because you save yourself so much time by hiring well," he says. "Changing salespeople is an enormous undertaking, one that often ends in failure and a great deal of frustration. You need to be incredibly thorough in your interview process. You need to ask effective questions—and you need to listen carefully to the answers.

Ogilvie continues:

You've got to get people to talk about job experiences—how they have dealt with various situations.

You have to find out how they conducted themselves over a sustained period of time in a work environment, especially when they encountered stress and pressure. Can they just roll with it when a decision doesn't go their way? Some people get so bogged down they can no longer function in the job. They become preoccupied with a single matter and fail to see the big picture.

I use a standard set of questions for interviews. The one that intrigues me the most is: "What are your expectations for this position?"—because it elicits all kinds of answers. It might seem like a pretty generic question, but it allows you to discover exactly what it is about the position that interests someone. When you start to hear, "Well, I'm really looking for a company that offers benefits," as opposed to, "This is the kind of career where I can work hard and accomplish my goals"—then I would tend to stay in recruitment mode rather than hire this candidate.

I ask candidates who are making a career change what they're looking for from me or the company that they didn't get at their previous job. That open ended question has a way of revealing what's at the root of their current frustration. When statements like "a manager who doesn't meddle" or "a manager who is fair with her decisions" start to emerge, you know you have someone on your hands who probably doesn't deal well with authority. If the response instead is something like, "I want to hook onto a rising star and get into an industry that has enormous potential. I want to put my talent to work in such a way that I can get my fair share of the opportunity." That's when you know you've found somebody who is coming to you for the right reason. They are moving *toward* as opposed to *away* from something. And that person generally brings much more to the table than the person who is trying to get out of a bad situation and find anywhere else to go. Interviewing well allows you to uncover this kind of information.

I trust you are jotting down questions to add to your own interview process. These sales managers ask them because they know what traits they need in a person.

Sarah McCann, my partner and wife, cuts to the chase with the first question she asks in any job interview. Sometimes she even asks it before she and the candidates have had a chance to take their seats:

"How's the job search going?"

The candidate's answer to this question instantly gets to the heart of their attitude. They don't realize that she's begun the interview; they think she's just warming up so they are not on guard. And their attitude about what is going on in the job market really matters. Some people bemoan the fact that nobody is hiring and that it is impossible to get interviews. They tell Sarah about how hard they have it.

Other people describe the process they have established to get a job. They tell her what techniques they are employing, and share which ones have been most successful. They also give her a lead on the attitudes of the companies with whom they are interviewing. This tells my wife whether her competition to get this potentially good candidate is going to be difficult to surpass or not. She can usually find out very easily whether they have a positive attitude, or if they walk around with negative thoughts when they are taken out of their comfort zone.

One of the things you are looking for in a sales candidate is an achievement history, since achievers tend to accomplish their goals over and over again. They are driven by the need to test themselves, push their limits, and realize increasingly more demanding successes. One of the questions that I ask a potential hire is this: *Tell me about the10 biggest wins you've had in your life.*

Achievers keep achieving. They need continual validation. Achievers collect and savor victories. These wins are peak experiences in their lives; they bring back a flood of memories and good feelings. When you meet a real winner, you will elicit smiles and enthusiastic descriptions of meaningful events in that person's life simply by asking about those 10 biggest wins.

But beware of the candidate who comes up short when you ask that question, as in the following exchange:

Candidate: "My 10 biggest wins . . . Hmm. I would have to think about that for a while. May I get back to you on that one?"

You: "No. I want to hire someone who can immediately recall their history of achievement, and wants to accomplish more great things going forward. You may have a minute to collect your thoughts—and I understand that you may be someone who has been warned not to brag. But right now, I give you permission to brag all you want."

Your job is then to listen to the list and elicit stories about the wins. You want to find out what compelled the candidates to accomplish the victories they choose to reveal, as well the obstacles they had to overcome along the way.

Ogilvie warns:

People will often respond to this by telling me that their greatest accomplishment is having their two beautiful daughters, or keeping their marriage together for seven years. While these are doubtlessly rewarding moments and accomplishments, I want to hear about meaningful professional achievements that you look back upon as a source of pride. I know that children bring great joy, and that being the head of a household is a significant responsibility. But why don't you tell me about your biggest accomplishment at school or in business?

What I'm trying to unearth with a question about school is any kind of innate desire to achieve. I am particularly impressed by an applicant who says something like, "Well, I entered college and the first year I tried out for the collegiate baseball team and I was cut. I was devastated. I was so determined to make the team I worked out at the gym tirelessly. I pumped iron. I shed 15 pounds. I worked hard during that entire year until tryouts opened again—and on the second tryout, I made the team. By my senior year, I was team captain.

Those are the kinds of stories I have to evoke from people to see if they have that kind of stick-to-it-iveness for a career in sales. I want to find evidence of their ability to persist in the face of adversity. I can teach them a sales process; what I can't teach is the ability to continue trying in the face of overwhelming disappointment—and doing so again and again. I have to find people who have the depth of character that allows them to handle a large amount of rejection and be satisfied with the occasional victory that punctuates the workweek.

Ogilvie understands he needs talent *and* tenacity.

There are other ways to elicit this kind of information from your candidates. "Tell me about a time you accomplished something on your own," is a personal favorite of mine. You are looking for the achievement, the obstacles overcome, and what drove the person on. Another good one is, "What are your weaknesses?" Matrix Fitness' Kent Stevens asks that question—not because he's actually interested in hearing about a candidate's limitations, but because he wants to hear how the candidate answers the question. Stevens explains, "It's when they tell me they don't really have any weaknesses that I take notice. Since we all have them, I have to find what they are covering up."

Or, maybe they are just dishonest.

A great question to ask during an interview is, "What was the last major purchase you made? And how did you go about doing that?" If the candidate's story involves online research, shopping multiple stores, and taking a couple of weeks before making a decision to mull things over—bear in mind that they are going to sell the same way. They will expect and allow their customers to buy the way they like to buy. These people have all kinds of deals stuck in their pipeline—because a competitor is in the prospect's office pushing them along and building a stronger sense of urgency.

Cliff Albert doesn't ask a tough question. Instead, he encourages a candidate to "Walk me through your process. Tell me about a typical day and a typical week as you go about making sales." The next five minutes reveal a lot of things, including whether the salesperson has a process or not. Albert explains, "I want to hear detail about 'how they make decisions.' A lot of times you'll get guys who just start rambling. And you've got to stop them because you haven't gotten anything."

Hire Slow; Fire Fast

Here's another question for you. What did you find out *after* you hired a person that would have meant immediate elimination had you known about it *before* you hired the person?

One sales manager revealed he had hired a former pro athlete who had sustained a career-ending injury. "I told him I wanted to do a ride along with him on Wednesday. We met at the office early that morning and headed out—except he headed for the bus stop.

'Is your car in the shop?' I asked.

'No, it's at home,' he replied.

'Well why didn't you drive to work then?'

'My license was suspended for a year.'"

It seems that there had been a quiet arrest for some cocaine issues that the candidate never mentioned during the interview. Oops.

There is one killer question that you can ask at the end of an interview that has saved us over and over again from hiring people with problems we don't want to help them solve:

"We're about finished with this interview; after this, I'll start my reference checking and due diligence. Is there anything you would like to tell me now rather than have me find out later from some outside source or reference?"

See what happens once you pose this question. Watch the candidate's eyes dart about in her head, and follow her thought process as this candidate reaches back into the past to see if there's any secret that they don't want you to know.

Make sure you allow one to three minutes of dead air to let the candidate think. And then get ready to receive some fascinating new information.

"Do you do drug testing for salespeople?"

"My arrest record is very short."

"If you call my last boss, you will find out that he fired me."

"I'm gay." (We knew anyway, we hired him, and he was a great team member.)

Interviewing becomes more difficult as the pressure you are under increases. There are three powerful tips that I can give you before your next interview that will keep you from making the typical mistakes:

1. Don't read the candidate's resume during the interview. Read it at least one day before and ask at least two other people to read it and point out any red flags or questionable statements for you to follow up on. You will be amazed at what you miss that two more pairs of eyes can see.

2. Have a set of questions that you ask everyone in the same order.

3. Interview all the candidates for the position in the same place with the same demeanor. Ogilvie cautions that it is possible to "go easier on a candidate you happen to like" rather than treat everyone exactly the same.

If you are not using some kind of validated standardized instrument to measure things like ability to learn, vocabulary, and sales aptitudes like achievement drive, organization, communication skills, assertiveness, mental toughness, probing skills, and motivation, you will lose more than you win.

Former Verizon Sales Director turned trainer Ed Fratz has the following take on hiring the wrong person:

There are good people who shouldn't be working for your company as a sales rep. Putting them in the field is a huge problem. It causes companies constantly to come in under budget and not hit their numbers.

Let's say a rep's quota is 40 (phone) activations. His first 30-days are a training program. Then, he gets a couple of month's ramp-up time. We want 40 activations. He turns on two his first month. He turns on four the second month and 10 the third month. Finally, he's on our six-month HR write-up process. HR won't allow us to put anything in his file until six months.

We finally get permission to fire the guy. Now we start the interview process. HR signs up a new salesperson. Now it's September. The salesperson has 30 days of training and two months of ramp up. That slot was budgeted for 480 numbers produced—and now it's under 100. We can't call up Wall Street and say we had a bad hire in Boca Raton. It's not so bad when you make one or two bad hires, but in my experience, it's at least 20 to 30 percent.

You now have some tools at your disposal for finding sales-people who can sell. Ask the tough questions. Select talent instead of settling for another *warm body*. Sales managers who hire just to fill the position or get the list covered will soon find themselves hiring that person's replacement.

Checking References in a World Where Nobody Will Tell You Anything

There is a short scene in the movie *All the President's Men* that can help you become an excellent reference checker. Robert Redford and Dustin Hoffman play Bob Woodward and Carl Bernstein, the young reporters who break the story on the White House involvement in the Watergate break in. In critic Roger Ebert's review, he wrote, "Who'd have thought you could build tension with scenes where Bernstein walks over to Woodward's desk and listens in on the extension phone? But you can. The *Washington Post* reporters had to check and cross-check their facts. Watching the movie today makes you realize the difference between journalism and the punditry that passes for it on cable news and talk channels."

In one tense scene, publisher Ben Bradlee, the editors, and the two reporters are in Bradlees' office. They are about to publish a story that accuses Bob Haldeman of conducting a criminal conspiracy from inside the White House and Bradlee wants to make sure they have enough sources.

"It would be nice if we were right," says Jason Robards (Bradlee). He asks the boys if there are any more sources to back up the story. After a little discussion, Bernstein says he knows a lawyer who was at the grand jury hearing. He makes the call and asks the lawyer to confirm that Haldeman was mentioned by Sloan to the grand jury.

Much drama ensues as Hoffman's character gets the lawyer on the phone. The lawyer refuses to talk.

At that point Bernstein uses the "I'll count to ten" ploy. He says he will count to 10 and if the story's wrong the lawyer can just hang up and they will kill the story. If he stays on the line, the story's right.

Tension rises along with the count. When Bernstein gets to ten his source is still on the line.

"You've got it straight now? Everything okay?" says the lawyer.

"Yeah, affirms Berstein.

The next day, the headline in the *Washington Post* reads "TESTIMONY TIES TOP NIXON AIDE TO SECRET FUND."

Of course, you are not trying to bring down the President of the United States. You are trying to hire a new salesperson who won't bring down your company's sales and your career along with them. Reference checking is a crucial aspect of the process. Past performance is the best indicator of future performance. Most companies have strict policies regarding how much they can tell a prospective employer (you) about their experiences with a former employee (your candidate). Sometimes you may not be able to get much more than the dates of employment.

One of the questions to ask a former employer is, "Knowing what you know now, would you have hired this candidate in the first place?" And not, "Would you hire her back?"

If the reference tells you that he can't give anything but the dates of employment, then you go all Carl Bernstein on him. Here's your script:

"Look, Mike. My job is on the line here. And I hope you'll help me as one sales manager to the other. So I'm going to count to 10. And knowing what you know now, if you still would have hired her in the first place, stay on the line. But if you wouldn't have hired her, hang up. You don't have to say a word. Counting: one, two, three . . ."

If that's too dramatic—and it did come from a film that won eight Academy awards—you can do what Sarah McCann does when she is talking with a reticent reference: "Look Marty, if I decide to hire her, what should I be prepared for?" Then, she hears,

"Well she doesn't get along with her fellow employees."
"She shows up late."
"I had a hard time training her . . ."
"She doesn't come prepared, and she doesn't take notes."
"I had to tell her everything three times."
"Everybody loved her."
"She caught on really fast."
"I trained her faster than any other employee."

Another way to get at the answers you want to hear is to ask the following: "Well—what were the best experiences you had in training her and what were the worst?"

You also want to get references that aren't on the candidate's resume. Toward the end of your interview, ask the candidate for the names of a couple of superiors, peers, and (even better) customers they have worked with in the last two years. I would call the customers first to find out exactly what they tell you about the candidate.

Here is all you need to say to the customer: "Hello, John, I'm interviewing Sarah Smith for a sales job in my firm. She says that you were one of her customers and I was wondering if you could give me any insights as to whether or not she would be an asset to my sales team?"

A customer's reference is a much better touchstone than a previous employer's because you get a sense of the impression that salesperson made or didn't make on the customer. You learn how that salesperson performs in the field. The customer knows much more than the previous sales manager about the candidate's real sales qualities.

Of course, if you're just hiring a warm body to call on a list or fill a vacant territory, you can ignore all this advice. But I would think you want to be known as the company that only takes the best candidates. You want to be in a position to select talented people rather than settle for someone who can fog a mirror. Scarcity is a good thing—and making the candidate jump through several hoops makes them feel that landing the job was a real accomplishment.

You want people whose best selling will occur in your customers' office after they have the job rather than in your office while they are trying to get a job.

Training and Developing A Players: *Miracle* on the Hudson—The Importance of Training and Retraining Good People

One of the feel-good stories of 2008 was the so-called "Miracle on the Hudson" plane landing. The event made instant folk heroes out of an airline captain and the crew of a downed U.S. Air passenger jet. Merriam-Webster's online dictionary defines a *miracle* as "an extraordinary event manifesting divine intervention in human affairs." It was not a miracle that a flock of geese flew into the airbus's engine, since that apparently happens frequently. After that, everything that *should have* happened, happened. The plane lost power—and **the captain's training took over.**

Captain Chesley B. "Sully" Sullenberger guided the plane to a textbook *water landing*. Sullenberger has his own air safety consultancy, and as an article on TheStreet.com revealed, "He had been studying the psychology of keeping airline crews functioning even in the face of crisis," according to Robert Bea, a civil engineer who co-founded UC Berkeley's Center for Catastrophic Risk Management. There is no doubt that Sullenberger is a hero. But without all of his training, he might have been a casualty.

Commercial airline pilots and crews aren't the only professionals who must constantly update their skills and continue to train until they retire. New York City Mayor Michael Bloomberg said at an evening news conference, "The FDNY, NYPD, and Port Authority police all worked together. They plan for these kinds of emergencies . . . you saw it in action."

Sure, you might be thinking, a trainer like me is going to try to turn a near-tragedy into a lesson about the importance of training. And maybe there *was* divine intervention. Looking at an airplane floating in the water is a highly emotional image. But if you watched the coverage unfolding, you actually saw hundreds of highly trained humans intervening. U.S. Air and New York City insist upon continual training and improvement. The airline industry was buffeted by last year's escalating fuel prices and this year's economic malaise. Many companies cut training budgets at the first sign of a downturn. Fortunately for those 150 passengers, skilled people were there to rescue them.

What about your sales team? Will they miraculously get better? Or do you need to keep training them?

And can you train them once early in their career and hope that they maintain their edge?

Here's a personal story that helps to highlight this point. Before I moved to Chicago and switched to tennis as my lifetime sport, I signed up for a three-day golf school. My buddy Larry is a golfer with a single-digit handicap who had won his club's championship last year. He's also the fisheries guy I talked about in the first few pages. And he was not impressed with my choice to receive professional training.

Here's how Larry put it: "If I were to go to a three-day golf school, Chris, I would have so many things to think about that I would probably get worse."

And what do you know? When I came back from the golf school's 18-hours of lessons in three days, I *had* gotten worse. I had 17 different swing thoughts, 11 of which started with the word *Don't*. For the next few weeks, I got progressively worse. I couldn't change all the things I needed to change at once. I couldn't remember and apply all of the lessons I had learned in such a short time.

Larry takes golf lessons. However, they are short ones—half-hour lessons once every couple of weeks during which he works on *one skill* with his pro. Then he practices that *one skill* on the range, and takes it to the course. Then he goes back and makes sure he's got it right.

Then he takes another lesson and works on *one more thing*—and so on throughout the season.

Whether you play golf or not, you can understand that taking a series of half-hour golf lessons spread over the spring, summer, and early fall will improve your game far more than one marathon three-day golf school.

Larry's approach to golf emphasizes—once again—that whether you're intent on becoming a great golfer or a great sales professional, your improvement is a continuous process—not a one-time event. Much like training for a sport, sales improvement is *not* about marathon sessions designed to get people up to speed and out on the streets. It's about constant, gradual improvement.

The pressurized water coming out of a fire hose can knock a person over. Too often we go into training mode and present a torrent of information. We have a limited amount of training time so we pack more information into it than our people can handle.

This doesn't work.

Think of learning as a faucet with a slow leak.

Drip. Drip. Drip.

Offering little drops or bites of information spread out over a longer period of time is the way adults learn and retain.

Do *you* have a process that helps you continually improve your people's sales skills and performance? Or are you relying on a marathon training session once a year or once at the beginning of a salesperson's career?

Why Sales Training Doesn't Work Like It Used To

At the start of a six-hour seminar, I could usually count on the fact that at least one person would approach me and say, "Chris, if I can get one good idea from this session, it will be a good day."

I was preparing to deliver a solid six hours of information—more useable information than any seminar these participants had ever attended. But most audience members weren't looking to implement 37 new concepts, learn 12 new behaviors, and adapt 14 best practices. Most of them were looking for "one good idea."

I kept shortening the seminar length, and increasing the prices. No one complained—because nowadays, people have less and less time to learn an increasingly unlearnable amount of facts.

That's right—*unlearnable*. Sound cynical? Actually, there's research to support this assertion. According to a white paper entitled "In Search of Learning Agility," by Timothy R. Clark, Ph.D., and Conrad A. Gottfredson:

> The growing dilemma is that we have long passed the point where organizations can expect their people to acquire and retain what they need to know to do their jobs. In a ground-breaking longitudinal study, Robert Kelley of Carnegie Mellon University found that in 1996, knowledge workers stored 75 percent of the knowledge they needed to do their jobs in their own minds. In 1997, that percentage plummeted to 15 to 20 percent. Finally, in 2006, knowledge workers reported that they only stored 8 to 10 percent of the knowledge they need to do their jobs in their minds.*

Therefore, the companies that rely on *boot camps* and lengthy classroom sessions to teach employees "everything they will ever need to know" are only falling, oh, 90 to 92 percent short of the mark.

It can't be done.

---

*To locate the white paper, Google "In Search of Learning Agility Clark"; www.astd.org/NR/rdonlyres/218AD515-A30C-40FC-BFB6-789AFE 9FFB9C/20059/Research_TRCLARKInSearchofLearningAgility2008.pdf)

This is another reason why sales training is too important to be left to the training department. They will look past the facts and keep delivering training until they can no longer stand in front of a classroom. Because that is what they do; they think in terms of hours of training instead of outcomes in the field.

The other mitigating factor in learning and training comes from the Bob Pike's 90/20/8 Rule. Pike—an adult educator who specializes in training trainers—claims that people pay attention for 90 minutes, but only learn for 20 of those minutes. Therefore, you must involve them every 8 minutes in a discussion or application of learning so that they retain more of the content. Let me break that down for you:

Let's say you do an introductory sales training course for new hires, which your training department tells you they can accomplish in five days. The day is 9 A.M. to 4 P.M., with an hour for lunch—30 hours, or 1,800 minutes, of classroom instruction. So according to Pike's rule, trainees are only paying attention for 20 of the 90-minute periods, which translates to 400 minutes of learning, or a grand total of six hours and 45 minutes. And this doesn't take into account the cost of feeding and housing this trainee, and possibly even flying him to headquarters.

This is a huge consideration. At one point, I had a British customer who spent upwards of a quarter million dollars a year with our firm. That's a significant paying customer. I would often spend seven weeks a year traveling through England, Wales, and Scotland conducting seminars for salespeople, managers, and even the company's customers.

It's a very nice perk in my business when customers become friends. This VP of sales and I spent so much time together—and he spent so much money with us—that I invited him on a short holiday in Bermuda. One evening at dinner we were thanking him for the business. He said, "You know, Chris, I paid you a lot of money. But 70 percent of my training expenses went to beer and beds for the salespeople attending your seminars."

If you've ever held an event in a nice hotel and paid $4 for a Danish pastry and $35 a gallon for coffee for the participants, you know how fast these costs can spiral out of control. Most companies that still have big meetings know how costly they are. For this reason, they often try to have marathon sessions by extending the day to eight or 10 hours to maximize the meeting. Then they wonder why nothing changes when everyone goes home.

There is a tremendous difference between *active* and *passive* learning. A salesperson who is involved in a 10-minute discussion about content will learn much more than she would from a two-hour lecture on the subject.

After conducting 2,100-plus seminars, I started breaking my content down into two- to seven-minute knowledge bites. This lets a salesperson receive the appropriate training on one topic as he needs it. This kind of just-in-time training is no different than looking up something on Google. If you have an important presentation to write—and not a lot of time to write it—it's probably more efficient to get a 10-minute podcast on proposal writing than to take a two-day seminar on it.

Learning today has to be ongoing, because there is more information than ever to grasp—as well as plenty to ignore.

Learning is a process, not an event. The sales manager who complained to me, "You have to tell salespeople the same thing four or five times before it starts to sink in," was equating training with telling. It's an easy mistake to make. After all, we get lectured by teachers and professors throughout our school years, and it follows that we start to believe telling *is* training.

My Epiphany

So what exactly am I saying here? In short: that the most important part of sales training is *not* imparting the information to the troops. It's letting them *tell each other* how the information works for each and every one of them. The meeting after they get the training is the critical meeting.

Here's why: The most important thing that ever happened to me as a sales trainer occurred early enough in my career to make a huge difference. True story: I had just delivered a 75-minute seminar to a standing-room-only crowd. They laughed, they cheered, and I was feeling proud (and maybe a bit smug) for the great job I had just done. A line of people waited to thank me. The ninth person in the line shook my hand and changed my perspective forever.

"That was a good speech, Chris," he says, "but you should know that we learn more at the bar after the speeches than we do from any of the speakers. That's where we talk about how your ideas apply to us and which ones we feel we could implement."

What a powerful lesson for me. The *real* learning occurs when people take the content they've been given, discuss it, and modify it to fit their own situations and styles. They learn more from that dialogue than they do from the speakers. It was a humbling but crucial lesson for me in my training career—and it prompted me to begin thinking about how to elicit more participation during my seminars.

That is also when I quit trying to get people to sell like I do and started getting them to think about small refinements they could make—instead of massive changes.

The Missing Ingredient in Every Training Program: Repetition

I like to listen to stand-up comedy when I'm driving. On one particular trip from Madison, Wisconsin to Chicago, Illinois, I listened to my Lewis Black CD, which I had already done five times. Yet surprisingly, I heard three jokes that I hadn't heard before—or at least, that hadn't registered with me until that moment.

I always like to ask people, "What are you reading?" But a better question might be, "What are you re-reading?" You can never get the essence of a book with a single reading. If you've read something that has made a big impact on you, go back to it 90 days later. You will find dozens of ideas you missed the first time through.

Why does this happen? Well, you read something, and start thinking about how it applies to you and your job. You wonder how you are going to implement that idea in the field. And all of a sudden, you've gone through a couple more pages without registering their content.

Watch a movie the second or third time and you will see scenes and hear dialogue you completely missed on the first viewing. Watch a DVD with the director's commentary and you will see even more of the film as you watch it through the director's eyes. You will see more of the layers of the film that you couldn't see the first time.

I know you don't have time to read, watch, and listen to everything three or four times. But if you want training to stick, you will need to embrace repetition.

For five years, I toured the country with a six-hour seminar called *Radio Sales 101*. It cost $101 and it was designed for brand new reps in a high turnover sales job. There was a broadcaster from Massachusetts by the name of Win Damon who attended the seminar five times, about a year apart.

By the fifth time, I knew him pretty well, and we were talking at the end of the seminar. "Wow, you've really changed this over the years," he said.

"Not really," I said. "It's about word for word the seminar it was five years ago, with a couple of different stories and examples. But the difference is that you're bringing a lot more experience to the lessons than you had five years ago—so you are getting different ideas out of the same seminar."

One more analogy to drive home the importance of repetition in training. There is nothing wrong with a high-school English class reading Shakespeare's *Hamlet*. It's not something to which a 16 year old shouldn't be exposed. But reading the play or seeing a production of it when you are 45 years old is a completely new experience because you bring so much life experience to the play.

Sales experience is very much the same. The more that you bring to a book on sales or a seminar, the more advanced information you will extract.

Buying the Wrong Thing: Bill and the *Magic Pill*

You may be a lot like Bill, a senior VP of sales for a big company. I am sitting with Bill in his Toronto office, talking about developing his firm into a world-class selling organization.

"Chris, we've held expensive annual sales meetings and invested in seminars and courses for our team. But what we're looking for now is a magic pill." All of the money his company had poured into educational and training initiatives had resulted in little change. This frustration is repeated over and over again. Corporate learning is either a competitive advantage or a monumental waste of time.

Now, wouldn't it be great if we could forgo the process of instilling fundamentals, and just have our salespeople pop that magic pill—one that would instantly embed the knowledge, skills, and attitudes needed to be a world-class sales team, along with the depth of experience to build trust and rapport with the toughest buyers?

It would be great. But simply stated—there are no magic (sales) pills or quick fixes. Oh, there are plenty of people peddling magic pills and quick fixes that other people purchase because they want to believe they work. "Let's fix it, and fix it *fast*." Plenty of companies would have you believe that success takes mere minutes. The truth is that any sales improvement process is like an exercise regimen—and neither is something you should ever start with the intent of *finishing* at some point. Lifting weights on January 2nd will not create any kind of lasting result; even the sore muscles will feel better in a few days.

Similarly, you add sales muscle and endurance by continually learning and adding new knowledge to skill sets. One speech, conference, CD, or seminar cannot change your salespeoples' lives. Real transformation takes a long-term, disciplined approach. Selling is a strategic process; for that reason, sales executives who want genuine improvement are waking up to the fact that sales training has to be a process, too.

Contrary to what you might believe, training isn't a reward. It's a necessity.

Let me tell you a story, because that's what I do. Since I sell sales training, I've heard hundreds of reasons why companies don't spend money on training. I mentioned the *Radio Sales $101* road show I used to do. I have conducted it for audiences of 80 people and 8 people; so, depending on the day, it proved be a nice cash cow.

On one occasion, a sales manager told me he didn't have the budget to train all of his salespeople, so he was having a sales contest to see which person was coming to the training session.

"You're going to send the loser, right?" I asked.

"No, I'm going to send the winner," he said, confused.

"But the loser of the sales contest is the one who needs the training the most," I said. "The winner should get weekend on the town or a prize that reflects the accomplishment."

He thought I was kidding. But I had never been more serious. And he failed to realize one very important fact:

Your salespeople won't develop themselves.

In *The Ultimate Sales Machine*, Chet Holmes quotes a *Harvard Business Review* article that states only 10 percent of us have what's called a "learning mindset." These people will buy books, subscribe to trade publications, and invest in online courses to help them sell better. The other 90 percent will only pursue learning and self-improvement "if it's part of a job requirement," he writes. These people spend their spare time pursuing a lower handicap or a higher score in World of Warcraft instead of meeting their sales goals.

Don't take my word for it. As you ride along with a salesperson or bump into them in the hallway, ask them . . .

What are you reading or doing to improve your sales skills and abilities?

Although some companies really do train their people, they usually do it at the beginning of their careers and never follow up. Training departments don't want to hear this—but training someone who has never been in the field selling is nearly impossible.

The most common reason for not reading books or signing up for a self-improvement program is time. "I don't have time to read. I have a family." The other big reason is that you have a lot of C students who find their way into sales. They didn't like studying and doing homework when they were in school.

That isn't going to miraculously change when they begin working for you.

No, my friend, you are going to have to make learning part of their job requirement.

You might even start implementing this during the initial interviewing process.

Tell the candidate, "This is a place to grow and not just a place to work. I expect you to read our industry trade publications and utilize the information services we purchase for our employees."

Or as I like to say, "Life is one big seminar, and lifelong learners get more out of life."

When you sell training for a living, you hear all sorts of reasons why companies won't invest in ongoing learning for their salespeople:

"We only hire proven winners," is one line. "They're already successful, so we don't have to train them. They bring their own book of business." This is the same mentality taken by pro baseball teams who go after high-priced free agents instead of developing their talent in the minor leagues. But you pay free agent prices, and you get free agent loyalty.

Another "great reason" not to train salespeople is that they are "veterans" who don't need it. This would be a great argument—as long as nothing has changed in your organization, your customer's organizations, the industry as a whole, or the process of selling.

But, of course, they've all changed. And your salespeople must change along with them.

Selling has gotten more fragmented for several reasons:

1. Every buyer is now only mere mouse clicks away from information about the solution to any problem she might have.

2. Getting past the secretary (how quaint) is no longer the issue. Rather, it is penetrating the fortress of solitude any buyer can erect with voice mail and e-mail barriers to entry. The mantra has become, "Try to get to me."

3. According research posted on Purchasing.com, buyers are having half as many meetings with sellers today than they were even five years ago.

Training salespeople used to be fairly simple: You'd buy a packaged program and give the salespeople a couple of days of instruction. Or, you'd have them shadow a more experienced rep in the field for a week to see how they do it.

Many potential customers have asked me, "Is your sales training for beginners or veterans?"

"Both," is my answer. "The beginners don't know it, and the veterans have forgotten it."

I was on the phone with the training executive for a Fortune 500 company whose employees always rank among the best-trained people in the country. This company flies new salespeople into headquarters and immerses them in a four-and-a-half-day induction course.

"How much of the training you do makes its way back into the field?" I asked the executive.

"Chris, very little of it even gets on the plane as they fly home."

The training director manages 11 trainers and the company has built a training campus at headquarters. These brick and mortar classrooms need a parade of trainees to feed the beast they created when classroom training made sense.

I have watched sales training become increasingly fragmented and specialized, and I feel that it's a lot like what has happened to beer.

The Driving Force of Division in Sales Training Today

"The Driving Force of Division" is the title of a chapter in Al Ries' book *Focus: The Future of Your Company Depends on It*. I like the way Ries thinks and writes about business and his specialty, marketing—and especially what he says about division:

> Like amoebas dividing in a Petri dish, business can be viewed as an ever-dividing sea of categories. A category starts off as a single entity usually dominated by one company. IBM dominated the computer category, for example, with the mainframe.
>
> But over time, the category divides into two or more categories. Mainframes, minicomputers, supercomputers, fault-tolerant computers, personal computers, workstations, laptops, notebooks, palmtops, file servicers. And more to come.
>
> For example—beer used to be beer. Then the category divided. Today we have domestic beer and imported beer. Regular beer and light beer. Draft beer and dry beer. Expensive beer and inexpensive beer. Red beer and ice beer. Even nonalcoholic. And more to come.
>
> You get the picture.

I have been watching the category of sales training divide over the past several years. I wanted to point out just a few of these divisions, so that you can determine if you need to work specifically on a certain area. Here's what I have seen.

In the beginning, there were the sales experts: J. Douglass Edwards, Zig Ziglar, and Tom Hopkins, to name a few. They would teach you everything you needed to know about selling in a day or two—sometimes a week. Then you were all trained up and ready to go out into the world and sell.

Then sales training divided fairly early on between business to business and business to consumer sales. Neil Rackham of

Spin Selling fame made the distinction between major and minor sales. Major sales were big ticket items requiring multiple meetings to firm up the deal, and usually resulted in a post-sale relationship between buyers and sellers. A minor sale was a relatively small ticket item usually sold in one meeting with limited post-sale contact or connections between buyer and seller.

After that, though, the division *really* started in earnest.

Executive sales coach Tony Parinello started focusing on selling to the VITO (Very Important Top Officer) and how to get the meeting at the top. Stephan Schiffman took off on Steven Covey's "7 Habits" to create the *25 Habits of Highly Successful Salespeople*. Advisor Jill Konrath works with small and medium business to get them focused on *Selling to Big Companies*. And Ari Galper is focused on making *Cold Calling* fun by finding out the truth instead of getting all salesy on a call.

And if you're afraid to pick up the phone? Well, there's a trainer for that, too: George W. Dudley and Shannon L. Goodson wrote *Psychology of Call Reluctance: Earning What You're Worth in Sales* and conduct programs based on it.

If you accidentally get the appointment, then more help is waiting; there are plenty of books on persuasion and the psychology of selling.

There are trainers who specialize in selling personal services like accounting and law. Lead generation expert Brian J. Carroll has written *Fast Forward Lead Generation for the Complex Sale: Boost the Quality and Quantity of Leads to Increase Your ROI*—an entire book about quality leads. We used to cover that in 23 minutes of a two-day generic sales seminar.

Have I mentioned *Sales 2.0: Improving Business Results Using Innovative Sales Practices and Technology*? It gets into CRM and selling with webinars among other things. Ann Miller will tell you how to sell using metaphors in *Metaphorically Selling*, while Richard Maxwell will sharpen your persuasive power by using storytelling to "pitch better, sell faster, and win more business." Then there's Bill Cates, the Referral Coach, whose book, *Don't Keep Me a Secret: Proven Tactics to Get Referrals and Introductions*, I like very much. My friend Dave Paradi has written *102 Tips to Communicate More Effectively Using Power-Point*. And to return to the beginning—Tom Hopkins is still at it. He's written *Sales Closing for Dummies*.

So there are sales trainers who will show you how to get a lead, or work on your cold call script to get the first meeting. There are others to tell you what to say on your first meeting, others to teach you how to follow up when your customers don't make the decision on the first meeting, and still others who will teach you exactly how to craft your Power-Point presentation when it's time.

If you think you don't have a prayer of landing that tough account, you could be wrong. There are books that have nothing to do with the sales process, which are merely designed to get you in the right frame of mind. I found one called *Time Out for Salespeople: Daily Inspiration for Maximum Sales Impact*.

Sales literature and sales trainers can quickly turn somewhat "New Agey" on you, as evidenced by titles like *The Law of Attraction for Sales: How to Connect the Dots to Get What You Want*.

You can see how the category of sales training has subdivided. So what *does* all this mean for you?

It means that there will always be more to learn about selling, because gurus—and wannabe gurus—are writing books about the subject faster than you can read them.

It means you may want to have an inside sales department that only focuses on lead generation and getting the first meeting for the outside sales team.

It *definitely* means you have to stay current and insist that your sales department be a place to learn and grow and not just a place to work.

It means you cannot trust training to one trainer, one off-the-shelf program, or your training department.

And it probably means we should abandon the notion that a salesperson is ever really fully trained. Substitute that idea with one that requires continual learning and improvement to be imbedded in the day-to-day routine of a salesperson.

There is more to learn about selling than anyone can keep in his or her head. For example, a salesperson who has an important negotiation later in the week needs to get just-in-time training on that one subject instead of trying to find the binder from the seminar he attended several years ago. There are as many pieces of advice as there are various situations in which salespeople find themselves. The good news: Someone has probably been there before. And if they haven't—well, then it's that person's job to offer the next bit of sales wisdom!

And to think, I used to have a six-hour seminar in which I thought I told people *everything* they needed to know! The increased amount of information and specialization in the marketplace means you will never know it all. But you always have somewhere to look it up when you need to know more.

The Coaching Imperative—Developing the People Who Develop Your Profits

We started this chapter talking about the difference between A Players and B Players. You can hire A Players. You can also develop them. Coaching is key and one of these Stage 3 activities that gets and keeps you out of the Sales Management Trap I introduced in Chapter 2.

There is no use in even bothering with training if you aren't going to coach people after the training.

Sales managers will frequently send a person to a training session and have no idea what he or she learned. Training that is not reinforced and coached will never gain traction.

Are you a coaching giant?

One Saturday after Thanksgiving, I went to Green Bay Wisconsin's Lambeau Field with my brother-in-law. There's a picture (somewhere) of me standing beside the 20-foot statue of Vince Lombardi outside the stadium.

And that's the start of the problem.

Coaching salespeople isn't like coaching athletes. While both activities might use the same word, they are completely different disciplines. There are very few sports analogies in this book, for good reason. College athletes practice 20 hours a week to play a one-hour game, whereas salespeople get a day or two of training a year—if they are lucky—and spend the rest of their time doing the job. While the word *coaching* conjures up images of Lombardi and John Wooden, this is far from the reality of the situation when it comes to sales.

Here's how easy—and how insanely difficult—it is to coach a salesperson. A salesperson walks into your office. "Got a minute?" she says.

"What can I do for you?"

"I'm having trouble justifying our price to the new buyer."

You knew this was going to take more than a minute—so now you have a choice. You can tell the salesperson what she should do. Or you can help her solve her own problem.

When I teach coaching to managers, I have a very simple exercise. One manager plays himself, and the other plays the coach. The person playing himself tells the coach about a problem he is facing, and I give the coach one rule: He or she has to ask seven questions in a row before giving *any* answers. Then, I let them work in pairs for 10 minutes and experience what it is like to be on both ends of this interaction.

The typical response from the coach is something like, "It was hard for me not to tell him what to do at first. But since I knew the rules, I had to really listen to him so I could come up with the next question."

Someone who is being coached usually says, "When I knew she was listening to me, it helped me articulate the problem and explore some possible solutions. Her questions let me come up with my own solution."

These lessons echo something incredibly important that Socrates said about 2,400 years ago—something that made an immediate impact me when I heard it: "I cannot teach any-body anything. I can only get them to think."

As one who supposedly teaches and trains salespeople, to sell that statement stopped me in my tracks. I realized that Socrates may well have invented what we refer to today as *coaching* in the workplace. This philosopher drew forth knowl-edge from his students by pursuing a series of questions and examining the implications of their answers. By today's stand-ards, Socrates would have been a coaching giant.

Now, compare Socrates' point of view to that of a sales manager who recently complained to me, "Chris, you've got to tell a salesperson something five or six times to get it through their thick skulls."

Time-starved managers and trainers try to teach information-overloaded salespeople to sell by telling them how to do it in a sales meeting or a seminar. However, if you believe

Socrates' assertion, then you really can't *teach* anybody anything—so these managers are already off to a shaky start. Experts speculate nearly 60 percent of salespeople never get any real coaching.

What most managers consider coaching is really one-on-one teaching and telling. When people start lining up at their doors and asking for help with a sales problem, there is a tendency for managers to *tell* them what to do instead of asking them what *they* think they should do. Many managers think that this tactic saves time. However, the dark side of taking this approach is that it conditions salespeople to come to them whenever they have a problem.

Instead, let's do some management training Socrates' way.

That exercise in my coaching seminar is to get managers to experience what it's like to be coached instead of taught. Coaching is the process of letting the person being coached— the coachee—discover an answer for themselves, instead of receiving one from his or her manager.

The coachee tells her coach what skill she wants to develop. The coach must then follow the seven-question rule introduced above: to ask a minimum of seven questions without offering advice. By the end of the seventh question, the person being coached usually has figured out how to proceed without being told what to do. An added benefit to this process is that since the coachees come up with their own answers and action plans, they're more motivated to implement them. After all, people rarely resist acting on their own ideas.

Managers who want motivated employees and increased buy-in simply need to decide to ask more questions. Coaches who complete this exercise report that they have to listen more carefully in order to move the conversation forward with questions only. In the second part of the coaching seminar, I get managers to differentiate between coaching and training. But instead of simply outlining the distinction for them, I have them work in small groups for 10 minutes or so and generate a list of differences. This allows them to catch themselves when they are in training versus coaching mode.

Recently, a group of managers created the list shown in Figure 3.1.

Training	Coaching
Group	One on one
New person	Experienced person
Procedural	*Ad lib*
Telling	Asking/Listening
Policy	Execution of policy
How to	Why to
Drawing from someone else's stories	Drawing from your own stories
Teaching skills	Refining skills
Rookie management	Veteran management
Done by anybody	Done by manager
Standardized	Customized
Procedural	Conceptual
Tiring	Refreshing
You are the process	Part of the process
Set time line	Spontaneous
Formal agenda	Flexible agenda
Proactive	Reactive (or proactive)
Specific goal	Journey to goal
Lecturing	Participative
Adherence/Compliance	Motivation/Commitment
Learning	Validating
Novice (New learner)	Pro
Develop	Developing
Black and white	Gray areas
One-way	Two-way
Providing answers	Providing questions

Figure 3.1 It is important to know whether you are doing one-on-one training or coaching.

Compare the Socratic method to the way most salespeople are trained, wherein the default mode is to lecture. It's a very easy—yet very ineffective—way to teach salespeople how to sell. Unless you are working with a complete novice, it's much better to get them to think about and discuss their approach. Asking your salespeople more questions is the way you start becoming a coaching giant. If I were there to coach *you*, I would ask the following:

1. How do you feel about Socrates' assertion that you really can't teach people anything?
2. Are there people on your staff you need to start coaching?
3. What might happen if you asked someone seven questions in a row?
4. Are you willing to try it?
5. What would keep you from trying it?
6. What can you do to ensure that it happens?
7. When will you start?

Since telling doesn't work very well, coaching is the fastest way to develop your salespeople and other staff members. However, if you think you're just too busy to coach, you might heed something else Socrates said: "Beware the barrenness of a busy life."

Making people feel like they matter and are important to you and the company is something for which you should *always* make time. A successful CEO once told me, "I have spent more one-on-one time with salespeople this year than I ever had before—and a lot of that was spent talking with them about their business. How much money do they want to make? How will they accomplish that? Offering my time and attention to them when I am in the building may be the greatest form of recognition I can give them. I don't tell them if they are doing good or bad. However, by giving them a piece of my day and showing that I do care, it helps them feel that I'm noticing and paying attention to them—and that they have value. While my sales managers can and should do this as well, I put so much pressure on them to complete other tasks that this might not always get done."

He went on to explain, "My advice to your readers would be to sit down with individuals and find out who they are, what they want to be, and how they want to get to be what they want to be. How can anyone give advice unless they know the answers to those questions first?"

In short: Sales managers need to be able to influence their employees' way of thinking. And unless you know what they're thinking, it is very difficult to do this.

As someone who has spent my career in sales, I have always loved specifics. All of my seminars aim to give people tools, forms, checklists, sample letters—anything that they can use as a model to increase their effectiveness. I've created charts like the Sales Management Trap that people can post on bulletin boards and office walls. I've provided the Commitment Tool so that managers can hold meetings with their teams during which they define exactly what they mean by *commitment*. And the following is another tool I think you will be able to begin using immediately.

VP of marketing and sales for Matrix Fitness Kent Stevens shared this form with me. It gives his regional directors a format for evaluating a territory manager's performance. The beauty of it, though, is that the territory manager (sales rep) also gets this form before the ride along. This shows the rep exactly what *good* looks like and how to score 40 out of 40 possible points on the evaluation.

This is an excellent example of lifting the veil and making job clarity totally transparent instead of murky and subjective. These territory managers are calling on the owners and managers of health clubs in their territory. This is like an open-book test. Of course, the company wants each territory manager to get a high score on the evaluation. They have documented that they make more sales when other territory managers exhibit the behaviors and traits being measured. You will, of course, want to edit and tweak the form so that it applies to your company and industry.

Sales Rep Field Training—Ride Along Eval

Purpose: The Regional Director will "ride along" with the TM on one of their business trips. This will give the RD an opportunity to critique the TM's overall performance. During and after the trip, the RD will review the performance with the TM and discuss strategies for improvement.

Measurement

1. **Preparedness** (10 points):
   a. Was the TM on time? Was hotel booked and within budget? Was rental car confirmed, appropriate, and in budget?
   b. Was the list of customer visits part of the TM's "Target Customers" or other profiled "A Clubs" (not small, irrelevant club visits)?
   c. Did the TM have web site or other profiling information on the prospect?
   d. Was there a local dealer in area that we traveled?; if yes, did we stop by to see them?
   e. Did the TM have sufficient literature and other support materials?

2. **Organization** (10 points):
   a. Was the travel route logical? Was the TM able to maximize time without wasteful backtracking across the city?
   b. Were appointments strategically spread out to minimize chance for overlapping appointments?
   c. Did TM have a map and list of other prospects to visit (cold call) in between the set appointments?

3. **Best Sales Practices** (10 points):
   a. Did the TM have a written outline listing the "minimum outcome and best case outcome" for each prospect visited?
   b. Did the TM prepare three to five questions that led to joint venture discussions?
   c. Did the TM do more listening than talking?
   d. Did the TM effectively tell the Matrix brand story at the right time?
   e. Did the TM refrain from giving the customer pricing or catalogs until requested by the prospect?

4. **Intangibles** (10 points):
   a. Was the TM dressed professionally?
   b. Did the TM have good hygiene (body order, breath, hair, etc.)
   c. Did the TM conduct himself in a manner that portrayed a positive image of himself and the company?
   d. Did the TM display confidence and the ability to take control?

> e. Did it appear that the prospect felt comfortable with the TM and showed signs that they could possibly do business with him?
>
> _____   _____   _____
> Sales Rep   Date   Total Points

The "Intangibles" section is an interesting one and requires more conversation—especially since professional dress will mean different things across industries. A relationship manager in a bank, for instance, will have different standards of dress than a territory manager selling high-end treadmills and elliptical trainers. I might add a couple of other judgmental criteria to this form, such as:

> f.   Did the TM look like fitness was a priority for him or her?

After all, you want your salespeople involved with your products and services. Do they look like people who use the very products they are attempting to get prospects to purchase and use?

Although you could copy this tool and use it today, I would not suggest doing so right away. Instead, I would recommend that you use this as a model and let your team create the appropriate evaluation based on their interactions, experiences, and needs.

Let's say that you want to do a monthly, bi-weekly, or weekly ride along with your salespeople to speed up your team members' development. You can call them together and ask them to create the criteria by which they believe they should be measured. After all, they're the ones who know this best.

What would be the consequences of holding a meeting and saying, "I want to evaluate your performance in the field so that I can coach you accordingly? If I were to ride along with you for a day, what would I want to observe you doing?"

You will then provide your team members with some categories for which you want them to provide details. Have them come up with 10 specific items under the general topics of:

Preparedness

Organization

Best practices

Intangibles

Instruct them to work in groups for seven minutes, and come up with 10 to 15 specific items. An hour-long meeting could generate dozens and dozens of ideas, and help your salespeople develop their own checklists for their jobs. After you reach 40 to 60 criteria, try to combine items to boil the list down to 20 or even 10 critical items. The point of this exercise is not just to create a form; it's to get salespeople to participate in the process of defining what *good* looks like in the field.

While you can certainly add your own criteria if they fail to do so, you will likely be surprised at everything they manage to come up with. Once your salespeople create the form, actually *use it* when you ride along with them. Observe whether they buy in to their own ideas and follow their own guidelines for what good looks like.

I love Kent Steven's form; it's a terrific model and a good tool for his team. You will like the one you make even better—since you're building your own tools with input from the people who will benefit most from them.

When you are coaching people about a specific meeting, the best time to do it is before the meeting not after it. You can influence the outcome of an important meeting by asking the salesperson at least seven of these questions:

1. What is your primary objective for this meeting?
2. What does success look like for you?
3. Where are you in the sales process?
4. What is the size of the opportunity?
5. What are the obstacles to getting the business?
6. What is one way to overcome that obstacle?
7. What have you done to prepare?
8. What questions will you ask the prospect?
9. What information do you intend to share?
10. How many members of the buying team have you identified and spoken to?
11. How many competitors do we know about who are going after this business?
12. Do you have an internal advocate and/or coach inside the company?
13. What action will you ask the prospect to take?
14. What is your fallback position if the prospect says "no"?
15. Is there anything else I can do to help you?

This is being proactive. Curbside coaching, having a *post mortem* in the car after a meeting, is coaching, but it is coaching that can't influence the result of the meeting. The more important the meeting, the more proactive coaching makes sense.

Mentoring, Mantras, and Management

Since we know that repetition works, I'll say this one more time: You are in the belief business. You have to know what your people are thinking so you can influence this thinking. Former CEO of Rogers (Canada) Radio Gary Miles told me about a question that his mentor asked him: "About halfway through my career, I was the General Manager in a pretty major market. My Vice President—who was actually a mentor to me although I didn't know it at the time—came through town and said, 'If you had a chance to do it all over again, and you could be anything—doctor, lawyer, politician, whatever you wanted—what would you choose to do?'"

Miles explained, "At least I was smart enough by that time not to give a flippant answer. So I said, 'I'll think about that and we'll have breakfast in the morning and talk about it.'"

"So, I actually did go home and [I] thought about it. I came back the next morning and said, 'I'd do it all over again. I would start as an announcer, and do all these kind of things—just because I love the business so much.'"

Miles then said to me, "[That's why] I think you have to have a passion for what you're doing. If you don't, then go work for the government—because you can work 9 to 5 and get that indexed pension at the end of it."

His mentor's question prompted Miles to ask himself exactly *why* he was doing all this work. He told the story to his management team years later to encourage *them* to go home and think about why they were doing the work they were doing.

According to *Mentoring*, a training film and accompanying guidebook from Crisp Publications, good mentors do things like "set high expectation of performance, encourage

professional behavior, confront negative behavior and attitudes, offer quotable quotes and trigger self-awareness."

Can you think of someone who has done these things for
you in the past? What did they do—and how did it help?

Miles' mentor triggered self-awareness by asking him
whether or not he would do what he'd done for his career all
over again. Thinking about the question and coming to grips
with the answer tapped into his deep passion for the business,
and made him even more committed.

A coach may talk with you about how you are going to
make this quarter's number; but a mentor will get you to delve
into the deep feelings and examine your life.

And all of us need both coaches and mentors. And you may
have to be a coach and a mentor yourself.

When I started my career as a radio advertising salesperson,
we sold commercials to local businesspeople. We often wrote
the copy for the commercial as well. I loved copywriting too
much and spent more time at the typewriter than in front of
the client. (Yes, I said typewriter. It was 1973.)

One afternoon, my mentor, Phil Fisher, walked by and
asked why there were 30 pieces of paper in the wastebasket.

"What's going on? You're taking a long time on that piece
of copy," said Phil.

"I'm having trouble getting it just right," I told him.

"Look, Chris," he said. "You write great copy. But your third
draft is only a few percentage points better than your
first draft. This copy isn't doing the advertiser any good sitting
in your typewriter carriage. Let's get it on the air and make
something happen. Okay?"

Phil was scolding at me in the best possible way. I heard
from someone (whom I simultaneously feared and respected)
that I was a good writer—so I started trusting myself more.
On that day, Phil Fisher confronted my negative behavior of

procrastination and perfectionism and gave me a valuable dose of encouragement.

I learned this valuable lesson in the span of two minutes. That it is still a vivid recollection nearly four decades later tells you how potent the mentoring process is. (Indeed, the very fact that I dared to write this book for Wiley with a five-month deadline is a direct result of that particular bit of mentoring.)

Most people consider *mentors* to be our elders, someone who is necessarily older than us. But one's ability to mentor has very little to do with age and more to do with the level of trust someone develops by being the boss.

You can be an "accidental mentor." When I was a fairly new sales manager, we hired a woman named Vickie who interviewed well. But once she was on the job, Vickie became unusually nervous. Before an important meeting or presentation she would rub the outside of her lower lip with her two front teeth, creating raw skin and eventually a scab. In one instance, I was sitting in the car with her. She was biting her lip and talking about how anxious she was about a call she had to make that afternoon.

I tried to get her to calm down. "Vickie, it's an important call; that's certainly true. But whether you make the sale or not, you still have your job here tomorrow. You're a good salesperson and I want you to relax and enjoy your meetings with customers instead of worry about them so much."

Seven years later, I met Vickie at an alumni event the radio station was having. She told me that those words were responsible for her "staying in the business and becoming a successful salesperson."

Meanwhile, all I did was point out the obvious and tell her she was good at her job. And that's what mentoring is. I didn't know it at the time; but you now do.

Mentoring is often unconscious. Miles didn't know that he was being mentored, and I didn't know I was mentoring. And if "accidental mentoring" works this well, then imagine what the results could be if you were consciously and purposely mentoring another person?

Here are four questions to get you focused:

1. What is the best career advice a manager or trusted individual ever gave you?
2. What course corrections did someone help you make that accelerated your career path and success?
3. What impact did someone who cared about how you were doing have on your success?
4. Which salesperson on your team needs the same kind of help from you right now?

Tom Clevidence—an HR legend in Cleveland, Ohio—has worked for some of that city's top employers. Larger brokerage houses, banks, and steel were some of the industries that benefited from his work in a 30-year career. At least two firms where Tom worked established formal mentoring programs that matched an executive with a younger employee. The mentor and mentee would meet monthly to discuss issues, problems, and successes.

Tom told me, "It was great for the mentee to get advice from someone with 15 or 20 more years of business experience. That shortens the learning curve. And once you have established trust and the person you're mentoring knows that anything she says is confidential, [you can begin to] work on issues." He went on to explain, "But I [also] got a tremendous perspective on the workforce by being a mentor. I was able to see what people two or three positions down the organization were facing and . . . thinking—which was invaluable."

Adele Lynn's book, *Mastering Mentoring and Coaching with EQ*, offers much more structure than I can give you in a single chapter on the subject. If you want to become more of a formal mentor, then by all means—read it. One of the most important questions that Lynn answers is, "Who to mentor?"

- Someone who performs well
- Someone who has the potential to grow
- An opinion former, a trendsetter, and a person who is at a node of interactions
- Someone who can influence others just by being who they are

That should be enough to get you started. Take just one person who fits this description to lunch sometime, let him know what you see in him—and that you would be happy to help him along in his career.

Mantras

Mentors offer quotable quotes. But if you use that quotable quote over and over again, it becomes a mantra. A mantra is a word or group of words thought to be able to create a spiritual transformation, like "Om" is for people who practice yoga. According to productivity guru David Allen, "The better you get, the better you'd better get." Repeated often enough, this statement reminds you that lifelong learning and striving is mission critical.

When I asked managers about their mantras, I got a lot fewer responses than I thought I would. But the ones I got were telling. "Deny the Drama" came from Dave Sturgeon, a general manager of Three Eagles Radio in Mankato, MN. It is very easy to be dramatic or emotional about a sale or lost sale.

But keeping an even keel is usually the best policy, making Deny the Drama a memorable, poster-worthy, solid slogan a quotable quote.

"Customers will not judge us by our mistakes, only by our response to our mistakes" is one I got from Rogers' Sales Manager David Shorthall from Toronto. Though it's a bit on the long side, it communicates the fact that *we don't have to be perfect—just accountable*. Those last eight words I just wrote are a pretty good mantra, too.

Matrix's Kent Stevens' mantra is "Make a friend today and the sale will follow." He wants his salespeople to come off as concerned with the friendship as much as the sale, because he's aware that strong relationships lead to many more sales.

"I'll call on you until one of us dies and I'm feeling pretty good," is one from legendary Wisconsin broadcaster Roger Utnehmer. It alerts salespeople that rejection is a state of mind. If you can have an answer or a last word to say to a prospect who doesn't buy, you can walk out with your head held high.

CBS Radio's Market Manager Rod Zimmerman's mantra is, "A car laid is a card played." Its meaning is simply that your word is golden. Always honor what you say.

Here are a few more that I have used in seminars and sales meetings to get you thinking.

" 'No' means 'not now.' "

Life is one big seminar and lifelong learners get more out of life.

"Selling is solving."

"People buy the WAY you sell before they buy WHAT you sell."

Education without action is entertainment.

You can open a book of quotations and find plenty more, but when you offer a quotable quote, it needs to be part of your belief system and something you will be willing to say over and over again.

The Secrets of Motivation That Motivational Speakers Don't Speak About

Motivation is another Stage 3 task and you want to make sure you have a solid grounding in what motivation is and is not.

I have never billed myself as a motivational speaker. For 25 years, I have conducted more than 2,100 training sessions for audiences comprised of salespeople and sales managers. But after one of those seminars, a woman approached me and said, "Mr. Lytle, you really motivated me today."

"Thanks," I said. "But I wasn't trying to motivate you."

"Well, you did. I can hardly wait to get back and try some of these ideas. I had written my resignation letter before they told me I was being sent to your seminar. Now that I know all of this, I can't quit."

And then she was gone.

Maybe I am *a motivational speaker,* I thought to myself as I headed for the airport. After all, the motivational speakers are the rock stars at the National Speakers Association conventions. They rake in bigger bucks for their speeches than everybody but ex-presidents, ex-generals, and disgraced celebrities.

Encouraged by this woman's claim, I began researching the field of motivation.

One of the first things I found on the subject was "Father of Modern Management" Peter Drucker's take on it: "We know nothing of motivation. All we can do is write books about it." Hmm. Not the most promising start.

I then ran across an article in *Harvard Business Review* claiming "job clarity is an important motivator." I reasoned the woman who told me I had motivated her had left my seminar with "job clarity." She knew, at that point, what to do and how to do it.

Think of your early days in sales when you didn't know what you didn't know. What you needed was job clarity. And when you finally figured out that when you do your job a certain way, you get a result, you were more motivated. It's like lifting the veil. The haze is gone.

Motivation Is a Breeze

Imagine you are a young trainer who is still excited about getting on an airplane. That would be me in the early 1980s. I got a call from a successful fast food franchisee who owned 23 Hardees restaurants. He asked, "Would you come to the Twin Cities and do some management training for my store managers and assistant managers?"

"Sure," I said. "What do you need me to cover?"

"Three hours on Wednesday afternoon," was his reply.

Most companies purchase their corporate learning by the hour and not the outcome. That is because they think about developing people as an event rather than an ongoing process. Though I digress, this is an important point. You can't expect much to change with one training initiative.

So the franchisee and I came to terms, and I did a lot of research on the company. I had a nice workbook and things were going well. I was two-and-a-half hours into the presentation, and was even allowing myself to think about heading for the airport. That's when one of the managers spoke up. "May I ask you a question?"

"You just did," I said. "Do you have a second question?"

There is someone in every audience who likes to play *stump the trainer*. Either that or they ask a question about a problem that they have let fester, probably by not firing a toxic employee, and see if you can (with very little data) solve it for them.

"How do you motivate a 16-year-old girl on minimum wage who could go across the street and earn five cents an hour more at another restaurant?"

Read that question one more time and see how you would answer it.

I had been to a seminar recently for people who conduct seminars, and the instructor had given us this advice: "When someone in your audience poses a question to which you do not know the answer, do not try to fake it. Instead, form small groups and let them wrestle with the problem."

"That's a great question," I told the manager. "Let's talk about it at your table."

She stopped me. "What are we paying you, anyway? I want to hear your answer."

The advantage of reading is that sometimes you get that one great line from a book. So I quoted one of the great ones. "Ken Blanchard wrote, 'If you can't describe the problem in behavioral terms, you don't have a problem—you're just complaining,'" I shot back. Then I urged, "What I would like you to do in your group is describe the behavior you are getting from this worker that tips you off that she isn't motivated."

"We don't need to do that in a group, either. She's lazy. She doesn't hustle."

Hustle is one of those baffling terms. It has as many different meanings as the people who use it. I used to run up the stadium stairs at my college 50 times after class to train for the high jump. In fact, I set the Baldwin-Wallace school record of 6 feet, 8 inches—which, at that time (1971), would have also been the women's world record. However, I competed in the College Division where I could take fifth place in the NCAA meet. That was good enough to be small college all-American. So I *hustled* and achieved some recognition. On the other hand, my friend Jill Lundberg worked out six hours a day for 18 months to prepare to run the Ironman Triathlon. Compared to her, I'm really not much of a hustler.

But let's get back to that seminar in the Twin Cities.

"I want you to talk about the behavior you would *like* to see from her that would indicate to you that she is hustling, and therefore, motivated," I responded. (In other words: What is the gap between what you're observing and what you would like to observe?).

A few minutes later, the manager stood up and had a completely different demeanor. She had stumbled on something and spoke much more quietly. "Look, this worker has to bus tables when people leave a coffee cup or a catsup stain on the table and before another customer sits down, or they will take their business elsewhere. She has to walk out into the restaurant to get to those tables. And I just wish that the people sitting at the tables she passes would feel a slight breeze when she goes by them. That's all I want."

"Can you measure a breeze?" I asked.

"They do it on the weather forecast with a wind gauge."

"I think it's called an anemometer," someone else offered.

"Or you could just put a paper napkin on a table and see if they can make it move."

"Let's try that now," I suggested.

One of the participants grabbed a napkin from the coffee service and set it on the edge of a table. Several people walked by the napkin, and we agreed to give the breeze a score of one if it didn't move. If it ruffled but didn't change position, that was a three. If it shifted on the table, it was a seven. And if it blew off the table, it was a 10.

The manager who posed the question answered it herself by describing the problem in behavioral terms instead of complaining.

I got a note from the manager saying that they had put a wind gauge in the back room and created a few signs that said, "Make a Breeze When You Walk By" and "We're The Hardees that Hustles." They trained their new people by putting a napkin on a table and rating the breeze. In short, they taught *hustle* by quantifying it. They created job clarity, and made their people understand exactly what *good* looks like.

You have probably already connected the dots, but "making a breeze when you go buy" is a standard of performance.

This is huge with minimum wage workers, and it is just as important with your salespeople. The use of precision language will make you a better sales manager now.

As a manager, you have to be very clear on what you want people to do before you can provide them with job clarity. A statement like "Make a breeze" gives you clarity; but the following statements don't:

You don't have a very strong work ethic.

You've got to put in the hours.

I need you to work smarter and harder.

None of these declarations enhances the salesperson's ability to improve—because even if they wanted to get better they wouldn't know how. Even worse, they worry about the criticism, but don't have any concrete suggestions on how to fix themselves. On the other hand, "Make a breeze when you walk by a customer" is a simple, observable, quantifiable behavior. Are your salespeople clear on what good looks like?

Be as specific as possible. This can be as simple as telling a salesperson to shine their shoes every other day or wash their car once a week, or insisting that the word *proposal* not appear on the front page of a proposal. You simply want the benefits of and the solution to a customer's problem.

Bottom line: Your salespeople want reasons. They need their leaders to use the word *because* frequently. For example, "I want you to polish your shoes and keep your car washed *because* people make judgments on you in less than two minutes based on appearance alone. And if you can't get the little things squared away, they will assume you can't handle the details of their accounts." Or, "I need you to use a customer benefit on the front page of your proposal *because* the first thing the person is going to do is go to the back page and see what the price is. You want them to have a benefit on the front page first *because* when they see the price they will go back and read the rest of the proposal to make sure the benefit is worth it."

I am about to reveal the final secret of motivation that motivational speakers don't speak about. Motivational speakers hired to address the troops rake in big bucks while secretly confessing to the belief that their speeches will likely create a merely temporary spike in enthusiasm. They understand that permanent change is a process, not an event. And yet, I've heard these speakers rationalize and even brag about their lack of long-term impact with the analogy that a shower doesn't last forever, either, but we still take showers. However, a shower doesn't cost $25,000 an hour. Nor does it require 100 or more people to fly in to take it. So the shower analogy really doesn't hold water (pun intended). For those of you who still hire the occasional motivational speaker, here is the secret of motivation that motivational speakers never mention:

Closing a Sale Is the Most Motivating Thing That Can Happen to a Salesperson

You've seen the swagger of a salesperson who has just landed a big order. There's nothing anyone can say to him in a speech or training session that can take him to that level of enthusiasm. Chanting won't get him to that level of motivation, nor will writing and making affirmations. Of course, there's always the fire walk. Once your people have walked across a bed of burning coals, they'll think they can do anything.

Unfortunately, *believing* you can do something and actually *doing it* are two entirely different things. The phrase *energized incompetence* seems to describe certain salespeople after attending a motivational speech. Don't forget the fundamentals. You can't just get them excited; you have to make sure that your salespeople know how to do the heavy lifting required to sell, including:

- Getting face time with decision makers
- Preparing like a pro
- Approaching and involving the potential customer
- Asking questions and knowing what to do with the answers
- Making compelling presentations
- Securing the order

Sinclair Broadcasting's Jeff Sleet confirms this assertion: "There is a lot going on every day and we tend to push fundamentals aside. We forget to teach the basic skills. Successful sales managers need to spend less time putting out today's fire and more time on fireproofing the team so that things are less likely to ignite."

Now you know: *Job clarity* and *achievement* are two powerful motivators. There are no shortcuts. When salespeople know what to do and then achieve this on the job, they suddenly become motivated.

Mark Peterson suggests that you verify your assumptions about what motivates your team:

> It's easy to assume that people [are motivated by] money. You have to know why they want money—but [the question is,] what are they going to *do* with that money? Once you have [the answer to that question], you can tap into that desire and motivation. You can remind them. Or ask them, "How's that college fund going? Have you got the down payment for that place by the lake?"
>
> Steven Brown's *13 Fatal Mistakes Managers Make and How You Can Avoid Them* provides the following wakeup call: "In all of industrial history, we have developed only three approaches for getting employees to produce more. Every motivational scheme falls into one of these three broad categories: Fear, Reward, [and] Belief Building. . . . The two most often used have proven largely counterproductive, because they generate short-term spurts of activity and do nothing to build the group.
>
> In short, sales managers must know that when they are using the first two options above—fear or rewards—to drive behavior, they are, in essence, using manipulation. And the consequences of manipulating include hostility and with-drawal in the case of fear—and an undue sense of entitlement in the case of rewards.

How to Motivate Salespeople without Hiring a Motivational Speaker

One person who *did* know something about motivation was American psychologist and business management expert

Frederick Herzberg. He claimed that, "Employees are motivated by their own inherent need to succeed at a challenging task. The manager's job, then, is not to motivate people to get them to achieve; instead, the manager should provide opportunities for people to achieve so that they will become motivated."

What follows from this assertion is the productivity loop, which takes into account three factors at work. (See Figure 3.2.)

The salesperson closes a sale and achieves. Perhaps there are high fives back at the office or a "way to go!" from the sales manager; but the mere act of closing will be motivation enough in and of itself. Salespeople may also get a commission or bonus over and above their regular salary for making the sale—another reminder in their wallets that they've achieved something to be commended.

There is another source of motivation: the satisfied customer. This is a driving force that smart sales managers take advantage of over and over again. A happy customer with a compelling ROI or a significant solution to a problem is the

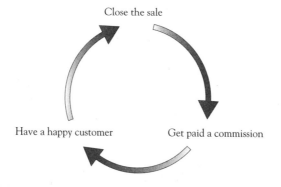

Close the sale

Get paid a commission

Have a happy customer

Figure 3.2   The Productivity Loop. Motivation feeds on these three events.

be-all, end-all of motivation. They give the salesperson a chance to say, "Look what we did for them! Their business is up. Their costs are down. They've been able to double their efficiencies."

We have an inherent need to help people and make their lives and businesses better. When your salespeople get a success story, circulate it through the entire sales force. Happy customers motivate salespeople in ways that you as a manager simply cannot. Since new salespeople don't have happy customers yet, part of your job is to make sure they are exposed to real, live, satisfied customers. One way to get this feedback is by inviting your customers to your annual meeting. Another is to have your marketing department interview and record (via video or audio) customers' experiences with your products and services.

Here's an idea to make sure you achieve one of the best sales meetings you will ever have: Ask your sales rep to schedule a "happy customer appearance"—either in person, or via Skype or conference call (depending on how your sales force is deployed). Make a rule that each of your other salespeople must bring three questions for the customer to answer. This keeps the customer from having to make a speech; he or she will simply have a conversation with your team driven by their questions.

How motivating is it to hear how you are helping a business? Try it and see.

■ ■ ■

My philosophy of sales training has thankfully evovled. For the first thousand or so seminars I conducted, I was trying to create hundreds of thousands of Chris Lytle *clones*. I actually thought I could get people to sell exactly like I did when I was selling in Madison, Wisconsin. Never mind the gender and generational differences, or unique personalities, schooling, and upbringing.

Never mind that the business of advertising sales has changed somewhat in the 35 years since I last sold a spot.

Once again, Bob Pike knocked some sense into my thick skull. Pike is the premier train-the-trainer expert. In other words, he does seminars for people who do seminars.

And I go to those seminars to get better.

I was sitting in the audience one day when Pike said, "At the end of your seminar, the audience members should be more impressed with their ability to do what you're training them to do than in *your* ability to do what you're training them to do."

Ouch!

Pike's statement was so obviously applicable to my own situation that I completely changed my attitude and training style—virtually overnight. And I realized immediately one of me was plenty.

So I shifted my focus to helping people become better sellers by discovering what they were already doing right and making small refinements in their selling approach to selling. One of the exercises I started doing in my seminars was something I learned from sales trainer Larry Wilson. He would ask salespeople the follow three questions, which I am also asking you to think about and discuss in an upcoming sales meeting. They are:

What is selling like when you're at your best?

1. How do you feel?
2. How do you behave?
3. How do your clients react to you?

I want you to give this some thought. Try to recall a meeting where you performed well enough to make a sale or get the next meeting, and see what you remember. It's different for everyone. Some salespeople talk about feeling relaxed, confident, prepared, and totally in the moment. They describe behaviors like making solid eye contact, walking tall, gesturing appropriately, listening closely, and using a confident tone of voice. Their clients react by giving them more time, sharing real problems, and eventually, buying from them.

In fact, you really don't need a sales trainer or a motivational speaker when you're doing your best. This exercise should help you discover how you feel, behave, think—even prepare—when you're at the top of your selling game. I couldn't care less about getting you to sell *like me*. Becoming your own better self is a more preferred result.

Give yourself at least 25 minutes to think about and discuss this. I believe you'll find that performing at your best is one of the most motivating things that you can do for yourself. The second most motivating thing is remembering those times.

Then again, I could be wrong.

Finally, Recognize That People Are Starving for Recognition

You want to keep you're A Players happy, productive and on your team. Recognition is one way to do that.

There was a restaurant in Newark, Ohio, called The Natoma. I started going there sometime around 1953 or 1954 with my parents and often with my Aunt Gertrude who loved taking her nephews out for an early evening on the town.

Angie Athan, The Natoma's proprietor, knew me from my days as a preschooler. While I was in high school, we had to house one of the visiting teams' basketball players in our home. After the game, I took my new friends to the restaurant. Sure enough, Angie came out from behind the bar and shook hands and welcomed me by name.

"Wow," said one of the visitors. "You're a VIP here."

I'm telling this story 43 years after it happened to me. That's how strong the memory is and how far a little recognition can go.

After all, as the famed television theme song claimed— "Sometimes you want to go where everybody knows your name."

In the 1970s, Plaza Hotel President James Lavenson delivered a famous speech called "Think Strawberries" (Google it), in which he relayed the following story:

> A number of years ago, I met a man named Dr Earnest Dikter. Maybe you know him. He was the head of [a place] called the Institute for Motivational Research. He loved to talk about service in the restaurants, and lack of it. He had a theory that I just think is nuts. Dikter believed that when you go into a fine restaurant, you are hungrier for recognition than you are for food.
>
> Now, just think about that. It's true. If a maître d' says to me, "I have your table ready, Mr. Lavenson," I positively float over to my chair. And after a greeting like that, the chef can burn my rare steak for all I care.

So what does this mean for your organization? Each of your salespeople has the need to be part of something meaningful.

In his pioneering book *First Break All the Rules*, author Marcus Buckingham offered 12 questions to which managers need to answer "yes" in order for their units to function to their highest capacity. One of the questions is: In the last week, have I received recognition and praise for doing good work?

Your salespeople are doing their jobs for reasons other than the money. If you think their paychecks are the only thing that motivates them—think again. After all, if money were the only motivator, one might choose to sell addictive substances.

The first step to instituting an effective recognition system is to make a spreadsheet for yourself that lists all of your salespeople. Then, put 52 columns beside each salesperson where you record one area in which you can compliment them each week. Then, build your recognition program around these three *Ps*:

1. **Purpose**. Your recognition program's purpose is to let salespeople know that you appreciate their contributions on a regular basis.
2. **Precision**. Recognize only meaningful and measurable facts precisely
   a. "You're doing a great job" is meaningless.
   b. "You've increased sales in Osage County by 7 percent in a month" is specific.
3. **Played down**. You don't have to ring a bell or throw confetti. Don't pile on the praise or overdo it. Simply voice your appreciation, pay your compliment, and move on.

It's important to do this on a weekly basis because it forces you to manage everyone and find something positive—despite the other events that might have occurred. It also lets you see what needs work.

Here's why this may be difficult for you: You're a middle manager. If you aren't receiving recognition from your own boss, you may not think that bosses are supposed to recognize their reports. And you will certainly not know firsthand what it feels like to be acknowledged on a regular basis.

Though it is certainly disheartening, that is not a reason not to have your own recognition program. If you need recognition or coaching yourself, then raise your hand and ask for help. Or call your boss and ask, "How am I doing? What can I do better? What am I doing right?"

Since that's pretty much what your salespeople want to know—tell them.

When was the last time someone recognized you? How did it feel? Do you want your salespeople to feel that way?

Recognizing people and making them feel important to you, your sales department, and the company is the fastest way to foster loyalty. (I revisit this in Chapter 6.)

When will you begin your recognition program? What roadblocks might keep you from starting? How can you overcome those roadblocks?

I end this chapter with those questions, which are questions you can ask at the end of any coaching session.

What's Changed
About Selling?

Massive Changes in Selling Have Taken Place Over the Years

"So, Chris, what has changed about selling since you started?"

A webinar participant once asked me that wonderful question—giving me a mere three minutes to describe 35 years of change. Besides the fact that there were no webinars when I began my sales career, I will share what I see as the three massive changes in sales that have taken place over the course of my career—and each of their implications.

Massive Change #1: The Internet

Your prospect can find out everything—both good and bad—about your company and its offerings before your salesperson walks in the door. The Internet has replaced price sheets and costly catalogues, and allows your customers to order whether you are calling on them or not.

Implication: Salespeople have to bring business expertise, not donuts and price sheets, to the table for every single sales interaction. Discussing how your product or service fits into the buying organization's strategic objectives is a starting place. Helping your prospects deal with change and get buy-in is another fairly new selling challenge, which leads me to my next point . . .

Massive Change #2: The Buying Team

There was a time when an owner or company president would decide, completely on his own, to buy something. Now the president wants *buy in* from *end users*. These stakeholders need to embrace change. And while it only takes one buying team member to stop the sale, it takes all of their support to *win* the sale.

Implication: A costly mistake or failed initiative can end a buyer's career. There is more fear and inaction in corporate America these days than I have seen in my four decades in business. From the salesperson's perspective, decisions seem to drag on. In fact, according to research done by Chief Sales Officer Insights, 90 percent of deals don't close by the time salespeople have projected them to do so. Wintstream's David Snodgrass confirmed this for me:

> We see slow decision making because authority to make decisions has been sliced; nowadays, you have to go to the top of the company to make a decision. And there [are price] considerations [involved in] everything. There's not a deal [that came to be] in which [you were up against] at least one to five competitors. Before, you would have none. You have to work three times as hard to hit quota as you did in 2008.

Massive Change #3: Information Overload

See Massive Change #1. These days, buying teams have access to so much information that it can be overwhelming. For that reason, the salespeople who add the most value are the ones who cut to the chase and focus on one or two key concepts and objectives. Salespeople must emphasize the ways in which their offering will improve buyers' business— not just highlight product specifications.

Implication: All of us have to do a better job of communicating and providing a strong underlying message. Metaphors and analogies that connect with a prospect's problem often work more effectively than long proposals and white papers.

Of course, these changes apply to different degrees in various areas of sales. Therefore, it's vital that you ask yourself: What else has changed in my industry? What are the implications? And what am I doing about it?

It's also important to keep the following in mind: Whatever changes we encounter—in sales and everything else—nothing lasts. Interruptions and disruptions are the rule in business. Despite this, however, the profound impact the Web has had on every business cannot be overstated—and is often underestimated.

Today, the thought of getting on an airplane to go deliver a speech seems borderline quaint. Why would you jump on a plane or pile into a car to travel to get some learning? Everything you need to know or find is online!

And I'm not the only one who feels this way.

A few years ago, I was on a plane reading *USA Today* and saw the picture of a Concorde Supersonic Transport (SST) sitting on a barge in the Thames River with Big Ben in the background. The caption told how the plane was going to its new home in the Scottish Air Force Museum in Edinburgh—grounded like an unruly teenager. The Concorde SST had flown for exactly 27 years. The fastest passenger plane in the history of aviation became obsolete barely a quarter century after its initial flight.

Interestingly, it wasn't a faster plane that took business away from the Concorde. It was the Internet. How, you wonder? Well, demand for expensive, fast international travel plummeted—and took with it most business people's need or desire to hold face-to-face, in-person meetings with their clients and colleagues. The Internet connects people quickly and inexpensively, significantly diminishing the need for executives to make a quick hop across the Atlantic. Instead, they can hop on the Internet, look people in the eye, read the room, and save $5,000. Big corporations rushed to invest millions in teleconferencing facilities to be able to hold these meetings. Today, we have Skype—which is free. Consider the implications of *that*.

All Change Is Personal

Let me tell you a story, because that's what I do . . .

I was conducting a seminar in Hershey, PA, for the Pennsylvania Association of Broadcasters, for nearly 400 salespeople and sales managers. During the afternoon break, a salesperson approached me, wearing a very sad look.

"Mr. Lytle, I am enjoying your presentation, but I have a unique situation in my market that is worrying me."

"I understand," I said. "Tell me about it." (I have never been anywhere where people didn't think they had a unique situation. Or that their market was different. Or that an outside person couldn't possibly fathom their problems.)

"Well, Walmart has just opened a store on the outskirts of town and a lot of my advertisers are worried about it. Some are even thinking of going out of business. I'm not sure what to do."

This conversation took place in the mid-1990s. By 1992, Walmart had 1724 stores and 208 Sam's Clubs. So the sales rep's situation was far from *unique*. Indeed, hers was an oft-repeated experience, as Walmart became the largest company and employer in the world—making Main Street a distant memory in many small towns.

Unfortunately, this Pennsylvania sales rep was suffering from a condition that psychotherapist Christina Maslach calls *pluralistic ignorance*: the idea that nobody has ever faced the problems you are facing. You are unique; therefore, your problems must be unique as well.

It would have been easy for me to give this sales rep a reality check by asking, "Have you ever been outside of your county?" If she had, she would have noticed at least a few of the 1,723 other Walmarts around. After all, they are big buildings, with obvious signs, in prominent locations.

But I didn't.

Instead, I shared a couple ideas and told her about a book on the subject of what to do when Walmart comes to your town.

There is an important lesson in this story that I thought about during my plane ride home: Change affects people personally at a gut level, and often blinds them to the plight of others.

All change is personal at first. And that is not going to change.

Flash forward 15 years.

The CEO of a company has hired me to address his sales team in January of 2002 at the company's annual sales conference. He calls to ask me to include some mention of the 9/11 attack on the World Trade Center.

"Put it in broader perspective for them," is how he phrases it.

I protested: "I don't want to talk about 9/11 in my presentation. It's hard to bring people back up once you mention that dark day."

"Chris, on September 12th, one of our top producers came into my office demanding to know, 'How is this going to affect my billing and income?'"

Never mind the dead and missing.

Never mind the bereaved families.

Never mind the impact on the stock market.

"What is this going to do to my billing and my income?" is the first question every salesperson asks when you change something or something changes.

All change is personal.

And all you can do—initially, at least—is provide information and listen to your people. You cannot get them to consider the big picture and the larger issues until they have grappled with their own reactions to change.

And that initial reaction? It's almost always denial. People cling to the past and want things to go back to normal. It doesn't matter if the change involves a terrorist attack, a terrifying little tweak to the compensation system, adapting new CRM software, or painting the sales office. There will be people who will wish for the old ways.

Because changing means shifting attitudes, creating new habits, and learning new things. While the old way may have been horrible, it was what they knew. The more people who know about the change in advance—who have weighed in on it and anticipate it—the less ramp-up time there is to get others to accept the change.

When you can involve people in the change process early, they will accept it more readily. Of course, when the change involves a merger or takeover, there are frequently reasons *not* to involve many people. But when you announce it, don't expect people not to feel blindsided and out of the loop. It takes time and leadership to build inclusiveness and trust again.

The King and You: Leadership Lessons from *The King and I*

Two tickets for a traveling company's production of *The King and I* cost $70; Rodgers and Hammerstein threw in the two-and-a-half hour leadership seminar for free. This well-known musical—which takes place in Siam in the 1860s—introduces us to a King of Siam who has sent for an English schoolteacher named Anna to instruct his 67 children. And while he wants his children to have a proper education, bringing in an outsider precipitates a clash of cultures, and the audience begins to see a man who is suddenly uncertain how to lead. He laments the changes that have occurred. His country is less isolated. There is more outside information reaching him.

There are more things to know than even a king can know anymore.

The King and I is a classic case of denial in the face of change. He has always used his position of power to demand compliance from his subjects; now, he needs to use a more humanistic style of leadership. He needs to solicit information from his subjects and involve them in making decisions.

Of course, he's still the king. So he won't ask for help even though his old leadership style is no longer working. After all, kings—and sales managers—are supposed to have all the answers. He's supposed to solve all the problems. That's just what kings do.

In one scene, the king asks Anna to guess what kind of welcome and entertainment he has planned for the visiting British dignitary whose countrymen have called the king a barbarian. When Anna comes up with a good idea, the king's only comment is, "Good guess." He then immediately implements her idea, claiming it as his own.

If you think you're the only one dealing with the stresses of change, you would be advised to see the heartbreaking price—literally—the king pays for not being flexible enough to let other people in the kingdom lead and give input.

Here are four leadership lessons from *The King and I* that—decades after its Broadway debut—still grossed over $70,000 for a one-night showing in Madison, Wisconsin:

1. **You can no longer know it all**. You must ask others what they know, and be open to listening to the opinions of people at the so-called bottom of the organization. They're the ones on the front lines.

2. **Leading by position power and demanding compliance works when the issues are small**. But in times of great change, you need to syndicate your leadership and get commitment from everyone.

3. **You need someone to talk to about the challenges you're facing**. It may be an outside coach or a mentor. But keeping your own counsel may not work for you over time. Even kings get scared.

4. **It doesn't have to be as lonely at the top as we sometimes make it**. Yul Brynner, who performed the role of the king thousands of times on stage and in the 1956 film version, remarked that the musical taught him something new about life every time he played it.

How the Game within the Game of Selling Is Changing

Today, these oft-repeated mantras are drilled into managers:

What gets rewarded gets done.

If you can't measure it, you can't manage it.

If you're not measuring it, you aren't managing it.

Good advice.

My high school basketball coach at Newark (Ohio) Senior High School was the late Dick Schenk. We were 22 and 2 my senior year, losing twice to the eventual state champions Columbus East. Along the way, we won our conference and beat Euclid, who was the runner up in the state tournament at home.

I came off the bench.

But when I came off the bench, all I wanted to do was get rebounds. Because posted on the bulletin board in our locker room was the leading rebounder per minute of play.

Coach Schenk preached rebounds per minute. "Boys, you can't score if you don't get the ball and they will score if you don't get the defensive rebound." RPM was the Holy Grail. And since we were being measured on it and recognized for it we focused on it and fought for rebounds.

What gets rewarded gets done.

So be careful what you demand and measure.

Bo Knows Winning

Bo Ryan is head basketball coach at the University of Wisconsin. Entering his 10th season as head coach there, he has already rung up five Big Ten titles and the six *winningest* seasons in school history. His winning percentage in Big Ten games is 0.713 and is higher than Bob Knight's 0.700 win percentage. In 26 years as a head coach, he is the 56th coach in NCAA history to reach the 600-win plateau and his career winning percentage is second only to North Carolina's Roy Williams among active coaches with 600 wins.

I lived in Madison, WI, for more than 30 years and have always enjoyed watching Ryan's teams. One day, I read an article about Ryan in the *Wisconsin State Journal*. It described how Ryan's assistants keep track of a very important *metric* during each practice scrimmage and during each half of every game, *points per possession*. In practice, the first team has to score at least 1.0 point per possession or they run sprints. On defense, the first team has to hold the scout team below 1.0 points per possession or they run sprints.

At every half time and at the end of every game, he wants to know what the points per possession were. That holds the key to the win or loss. Since every team gets the ball an equal number of times during the game, this *metric* is the best indicator of performance of both the offense and the defense.

It doesn't matter if the game is a fast-paced freewheeling affair or a deliberate game where the team chews up the 35 seconds on every offensive possession; the points per possession metric always holds true. If you score 1.2 points per possession and hold your opponent to 0.95 points per possession, you win every game. Every single player understands the importance of the measurement.

Bo Ryan teaches his players to win basketball by showing them how to win the *game within the game* of basketball. By measuring points per possession, he makes winning every possession a new game. Since people know that is what they are being measured on, they bring energy and focus to each possession.

The Missing Metrics

You have a sales team, not a basketball team. But what you measure matters. What you rant about is what members of your sales team pay rapt attention to. You already track the obvious metrics that lead to sales:

- Number of first meetings
- Number of opportunities in the pipeline
- Amount of dollars in the pipeline
- Closing ratio

- Length of the selling cycle
- Percentage of sales to goal

But I challenge you to measure three *missing metrics* that very few sales managers think about. If you ask about these during every sales meeting and every one-on-one session with your salespeople, they will understand how to win the game within the game of selling.

- Relationship metrics
- Sales process metrics
- Engagement metrics

Relationship Metrics

Your last meeting *is* the relationship. In today's sped up world, your prospects go from meeting to meeting and rarely think of your salespeople unless they are in front of them or on the phone with them.

How strong are your relationships? The answer can be found by rating the quality of your last meeting using "The Chart." In *The Accidental Salesperson*, I introduced "The Chart." It is my attempt to measure the strength of the relationship you are having with a buyer or a customer. Moreover, it is designed to help you plan a higher quality meeting with the buyer or buying team.

Feel free to add your own criteria to "The Chart." But first, look at my ideas for Level 1, 2, 3, and 4 meetings. (See Figure 4.1.)

Here's a hypothetical question worth pondering: Would you rather have your salespeople make 10 Level 1 calls or 5 Level 2 calls?

	Level 1	Level 2	Level 3	Level 4
Level of Trust	Neutral or distrustful	Some credibility	Credible to highly credible; based on salesperson's history	Complete trust based on established relationships and past performance
Goal/Call Objective	To open doors; to "see what's going on"	To persuade and make a sale or to advance the prospect through the process	Customer creation and retention; to "find the fit"; to upgrade the client and gain more information	To continue upgrading and increase share of business
Approach and Involvement	Minimal or nonexistent	Well-planned; work to get prospect to buy into the process	True source of industry information and "business intelligence"	Less formal and more comfortable because of trust and history
Concern or Self-Esteem Issue	Being liked	Being of service, solving a problem	Being a resource	Being an "outside insider"
Pre-Meeting Preparation	Memorize a canned pitch or "wing it"	Set call objectives; pre-script questions; articulate purpose–process–payoff	Research trade magazines, Internet; analyze client's competition	Through preparation, sometimes with proprietary information unavailable to other reps
Presentation	Product literature, spec sheets, rate sheets	Product solution for problem they uncover during needs analysis	Systems solutions	Return on investment proof and profit improvement strategies
Point of Contact	Buyer or purchasing agent	End users as well as buyer or purchasing agent	Buyers, end users, and an "internal coach" or advocate within client's company	"Networked" through the company; may be doing business in multiple divisions

DEFAULT ▲ PREFERENCE SETTINGS

Figure 4.1   Analyze your last meeting with the chart to gauge the level of the relationship.

The Chart measures the quality of the meeting your salesperson is planning to have or that he just had. Does the quality of the call matter?

You probably have already observed that the very best producers are not necessarily making the most calls. But they are the ones who get the most out of every call they make.

Figure 4.2 Phases of the Selling Process

In a complex sale, the pre-meeting planning and customer research win the day. And that takes time away from running around furiously making calls.

Sales Process Metrics

There are many ways to imagine a sales process. (See Figures 4.2 and 4.3.) The funnel seems to be the most popular. Too often, salespeople fail to make the distinction between real and imagined prospects. In my sales process, I refer to leads and targeted accounts as people at companies with whom I would like to meet. Until there is a first meeting and a scheduled second meeting, they are neither prospects nor opportunities. In fact, I recommend that you not put anything into your projections until the presentation phase is over and a decision date is planned.

The graphic in Figure 4.2 portrays the distinct stages of a complex sale. It's important to look at what happens as your salespeople try to get their clients through the funnel and out the tiny end where the dollars are. There's always a

Figure 4.3   Phases of the Selling Process

chance that the first meeting may be the last meeting. But if your salespeople get a second or third scheduled meeting, they've moved the sale into the Information phase. This is where you are gathering information about the customer's problem, and they are doing their due diligence with regard to your solution.

The Presentation phase is where you can begin to think about putting a prospect in your projections. Here, you have made a specific recommendation with a timetable and asked for a specific dollar amount.

Once a salesperson has presented and asked for the business, it would be nice if the person across the desk could give you a decision. If that happens in your business, great. But more often than not, the Presentation phase occurs at the end of your sales process. However, it is often seen by buyers as simply the middle—certainly not the end—of the buying process. The buying committee members discuss the options *ad nauseam*, while the CFO and CEO—who have

not been in the meetings, but may have stayed in the loop—
vet the decision.

If you ask, your key contact can likely tell you about his
particular organization's buying process. If you want your
pipelines to be as pristine as possible, you need to be aware of
this timetable and decision-making process in order to coach
your people through it.

I recommend tracking sales process metrics, or *new business
moves*. You are trying to get on the prospect's radar—and
eventually on her calendar for a first meeting. The following
are some tactics that might lead to that first meeting:

- Seed the prospect with an article or whitepaper
- Write a snail mail letter that offers a benefit or solution, or touts a success story from a reference
- Get a referral from a current customer
- Invite the prospect to a company webinar or live event
- Dial the phone and leave 7 to 14 voice mails with the company's messaging system
- Have the first phone conversation
- Book the first meeting
- Find out what the prospect is trying to accomplish or the problem she is trying to solve
- Demonstrate an understanding of the issue
- Demonstrate capability in your area and industry, especially in terms of the prospect's particular problem(s)
- Write a proposal
- Deliver the proposal
- Ask for the business
- Wait for the buying team to make a decision

- Work the expiration date of your proposal
- Close the deal

Your own process may be extremely simpler or elaborately more complex. You may have salespeople assigned to one or two strategic accounts, or have them covering 50 different prospects and customers per territory. These salespeople may be at various stages of the sales process with a dozen or more accounts.

So rather than simply focusing on calls, encourage salespeople to concentrate on the next step in the process. Measure how many new business moves they made in a week. In lieu of an order, you can still see the progress they make when they advance prospects along in the sales process. Your salespeople may have made a dozen new business moves with no orders to show for them yet. But you can see—and celebrate—other kinds of movement. One standard to establish is to track how many new business moves a salesperson needs to make in order to succeed. Of course, you can find this out by seeing what is actually going on with the top third of your team.

Now you are now coaching the game within the game of selling. You aren't yelling and screaming about the score. You are focusing your team on the activities that lead to the score. You are counting the things that count instead of simply demanding that people *make more calls.*

Engagement Metrics and Performing Sales Pipeline Angioplasty on Your Salespeople's Individual Pipelines

You can measure the quality of the meeting. You can count the number of new business moves a salesperson has made.

Now I want to introduce you to a leading indicator of sales performance: Engagement Metrics.

I define engagement metrics as the number of prospects who have one of your salespeople on **their calendars** for a next step.

Engaged prospects move the sale along when salespeople aren't in front of them. They hold meetings with their team to discuss your products and services.

The Epidemic

Dead and dying deals are currently clogging your salespeople's pipelines. Sales that drag on too long drag down salespeople's efficiency—as does spending time, energy, and resources on deals that are already dead. In medicine, an angioplasty is a procedure that opens coronary arteries that have been clogged by the fatty plaque buildup associated with coronary artery disease. Despite the fact that heart disease is thankfully starting to decline in the United States, the incidence of clogged sales pipelines is increasing at alarming rates. Chief Sales Officer *Insights*, conducted major survey of 1,337 chief sales officers reveals that 54 percent of forecasted deals don't close (30 percent go to a competitor; 24 percent go to no decision. The same survey found that 90 percent of the deals don't close when forecasted. It would appear that "Dismal pipeline analysis is the rule.")

Sales pipeline angioplasty is the ongoing process of methodically eliminating dead deals and reengaging with real prospects who have quit returning your salespeople's phone calls. One immediate outcome of this process is new movement of real opportunities through healthier sales pipelines.

Other indications of a successful procedure are shorter sales cycles and more accurate projections.

Warning Signs of Clogged Pipelines

The first warning sign is that you're reading this chapter, and are biting your nails wondering if the following list will apply to you and your company. Here are seven more warning signs that your company is a candidate for sales pipeline angioplasty:

1. You find it hard to make accurate forecasts based on the information you get from your salespeople.
2. Too much of your forecast is based on subjective information.
3. When you finally learn about lost opportunities, it's too late for management to intervene and save the sale.
4. You find yourself putting out fires instead of proactively developing your salespeople.
5. Your salespeople are "too busy" reacting to current customers to make efforts toward prospecting and new business acquisitions.
6. You find it difficult to assess the kind of effort of your salespeople are making.
7. You don't have a *distant early warning system* to alert you that a salesperson needs help before he or she actually asks for it.

Your salespeople are busy. But this *busyness* no longer equates to actually achieving business gains. You may have already noticed that your salespeople seem to be working harder than ever with less to show for it. They face long, drawn-out sales cycles and the need to please multiple decision makers. At the same time, they waste countless hours pursuing information seekers instead of real prospects. They may even tell you that sales are imminent, despite the fact that prospects have quit returning their calls. Amazingly, they remain optimistic when pessimism and facing the brutal truth are what's called for.

The number of scheduled meetings with high-value prospects is the **leading indicator** of the health of your company's sales pipelines. The number of prospects who have your salespeople *on their calendars* is the third **missing metric**. Engaged customers do things for you within their own companies to move the buying process forward.

Engagement metrics are mission critical today. Measuring the number of scheduled meetings on your salespeople's calendar is the missing metric that most managers need to get a handle on and manage—because **increasing the number of scheduled meetings is the surest way to increase sales.** It's a more powerful and accurate metric than the old standby—the number of sales calls.

Here's why: One day, I was going over the *call reports* of a client company, one of which had the following three-sentence notation: "Went to see Ed at _XYZ_ Company. He was having lunch with another vendor at Happy Joe's Pizza. Will call again next Tuesday afternoon." That salesperson had dutifully detailed a meeting that never occurred—and took three sentences to do it. This so-called sales call involved driving 30 miles to see a person who wasn't available. When I asked the sales rep who submitted the call report why she had gone to the trouble to document it, she informed me that her boss required her to make 10 calls a day—and that was one of them.

Your company may have already invested heavily in a CRM or Sales Force Automation program to gather *critical* sales data. However, these frequently become repositories for marginally useful and *cover my butt* notes. Sales executives and field sales managers spend far too many evening hours and weekends wading through this kind of detail:

- "Left voice mail."
- "Left second voice mail."
- "Sent catalogue."
- "E-mailed prospect about our new pricing."
- "Reached assistant. Prospect is traveling on business. Call in a week."
- "Called Pat, but he was on his way upstairs and couldn't come to the phone."

Real sales come from *real meetings*—whether in person, online, or on the phone. There is no need to write a sentence about dialing the phone and not reaching the intended party. This time would be better spent dialing another prospect and setting up an actual meeting. Salespeople who put opportunities into their projections at 50, 75, or 90 percent without having a next meeting are fooling themselves and attempting to fool their bosses. A good meeting is one that ends with a next step on the potential customer's calendar. Salespeople need to ask for specific commitments from potential customers. However, they're afraid to seem pushy, and often mistake friendliness and expressed interest for buying signals.

So . . . what deep dark secrets are lurking in your sales pipeline?

There's an even better question: **Why should there be any secrets lurking in any salesperson's pipeline?** And why should you have to spend evenings and weekends trying to decode call reports to figure out what's really happening?

After all, next quarter's sales results are already predetermined by this quarter's pipeline health. Can you tell how these are shaping up now? How about the quarter after that?

Jack Nicholson's classic line from *A Few Good Men* explains exactly why these projections are so wacky: *You can't handle the truth.*

Your salespeople can't handle it when they bring you bad news and you roll your eyes and let out the heavy sighs.

So they tell you lies. They tell you everything is fine just to shut you up.

And it *works.*

But you can't let it work anymore. You've got to be relentless at getting at the real truth without judging the person.

There are various reasons why sales pipelines are clogged. Fortunately, there are also many ways to start performing sales pipeline angioplasty on each one of them.

Before you include an item into the projections that you send to your CFO, make sure your sales rep has planned a next step. Has the salesperson asked the critical question, "When are you planning to make a decision?" Or, "How soon do you want to address this problem?" Just because there is a proposal and pricing on the table doesn't make this a sure thing. As Chief Sales Officer Insight principle Jim Dickey says, "No customer ever buys 75 percent of a deal. It's usually all or nothing."

Again, *engagement metrics* refer to the number of prospects and customers who have your salespeople on their calendars for a scheduled next action step. This is a leading indicator of the likelihood that they will buy. Most decisions to purchase do not occur when your salespeople are in front of the customer. Instead, prospects hold another one of the famed *meeting after the meeting* with the buying team, and have a discussion about implementing your plan. This happened to you when you were in sales and it happens to your salespeople on a daily basis.

Here's a scenario that's repeated over and over again; One of your sellers is in front of a prospect or several prospects from the buying team. There is lots of leaning forward, nodding, and eye contact. The buying team members ask pointed questions. The salesperson answers them flawlessly.

And then it happens.

The point person looks at his watch and says, "I've got to jump on a conference call, everyone. This has been great. Let's continue this conversation after the long holiday weekend. Can you call me next Tuesday to set that up?"

And, of course, because he wants to be polite and doesn't want to ruin the moment, the salesperson agrees.

On the following Tuesday, the calling process begins. And for some impossible to fathom reason, the formerly excited prospect neither takes nor returns the call.

This can go on for days, and even weeks. And it will— unless you teach every single one of your salespeople to use the following response and the *magic question*: "I would be happy to call you next Tuesday. Are you willing to work with me on a calendar basis?"

There are only two answers:

1. Yes, absolutely, let's get this on the calendar. Does 9:15 A.M. work for you?
2. No, I've got to go. Just call me.

And variations of the same.

Here are two foolproof definitions that will make your projections a source of pride instead of frustration.

- A *prospect* is someone who is willing to engage with you on a calendar basis. Engaged prospects and customers do things for you within their own companies to move the buying process forward.

- An *information seeker* is a person who lets you chase him and possibly pin him down later for a next step.

Never put an information seeker into your projections. Your salespeople will use words like *slam dunk, hot prospect,* and *no brainer.* You do not know or allow these words. In fact, they should make you suspicious when used.

"What is the next step?" you ask. "Is that step on their calendar now or not?" There are prospects and information seekers—end of story. End of ridiculous and fruitless projections.

Regardless of the length of your sales cycle—and I'm betting it's both longer than you'd like it to be and longer than it was last year—you need to be aware of who has your salespeople on their calendars for a next step.

So, start inspecting their calendars instead of just reading their call reports. Count the number of meetings they have scheduled over the next two weeks; increasing these is the fastest way to increase sales. It is a more powerful and accurate metric than the number of sales calls someone intends or pretends to have made.

The Magic E-Mail

When a customer didn't call me back, I sent the following *magic e-mail* to get stalled deals moving and dead deals out of my sales pipelines:

Subject: Quick Question

"Cliff, I still have you on my 'waiting for' list of people I'm expecting to hear from. Am I still on your radar? Chris"

His response:

"You are good. Let's talk this morning if you are available. I'm out of town but can be reached on my cell phone."

Result: Before I could call him, he called me from the road and we scheduled our next meeting. My two-sentence e-mail worked (I believe) because I really do have a *waiting for* list and keep track of people with whom I have pending business who call me back.

Thousands of salespeople on three continents are already using this e-mail to get answers. Reengagement happens time after time. Even getting a "No" can be considered a success, since this gets the deal out of your pipeline and projections and lets your salespeople focus their energy on new and real opportunities.

The e-mail works because the subject line, "Quick Question" is the most effective one I've ever used. The typical business person experiences 170 to 190 different interactions per day, and is in a state of chronic preoccupation. This means that they are usually so busy thinking about what they *aren't* doing that they can't focus on what they *are* doing.

You may well be able relate.

The "Quick Question" subject line gives these professionals —with their lack of time and short attention spans— something easy and quick to do. There is no 23-page PDF attached to the e-mail that they have to read; it's a simple request. They can act on it and get on with their crazy busy days.

Massive changes in selling mean you need to measure more than calls. The three missing metrics are a good place to start. Of course, you have already decided to teach everyone about "The Magic E-Mail." Get salespeople to identify their stalled deals and send The Magic E-Mail to everyone who is stalling or has seemingly disappeared completely.

You will be pleasantly surprised. But I won't be.

I use it several times a week to keep my own pipeline pristine.

Running Great Sales Meetings Every Time

S ales meetings are your chance to break through to the whole team and make a lasting leadership impact. Conversely, sales meetings are your chance to look unprepared and uninspiring.

Think about that every time you call a sales meeting.

The inside joke that professional speakers crack at our conventions goes something like this: "It is easier to get a new audience than come up with a new speech."

I'm here all week. Please tip your servers.

So it might not be a very funny joke to you, but it's very true—and an idea you need to keep in mind when you plan and run your sales meetings. You have to come up with fresh content each week, or you risk running the most boring meetings in the world.

Accomplished sales manager—and my wife—Sarah McCann recalls, "I used to plan my Monday morning sales meeting while I was watching 60 Minutes on Sunday night— or worse yet, while I was driving to the office to conduct it." Garfield Ogilvie puts it this way:

> The challenge for sales managers is that they are a limited source of content. We work with our salespeople and share our points of view with them all week. So there is a limit on how much more an individual has to offer. My coaching— whether it's in the car or in the sales office—calls upon my perspective and experience. And while I'm well-read, competent, and rich in knowledge, there's only so much material I can use before I start repeating myself. And if there's anything

that turns off an audience, it's "Well, I've heard all that before."

By now, you are getting used to asking questions instead of giving all of the answers. If you were sitting in my office today, I would ask you three questions about your sales meetings:

1. Would your salespeople attend if your meetings were optional?
2. Would they gladly pay if you charged five dollars an hour for attendance? Because attending your sales meetings puts money in their pockets in the form of increased sales.
3. Would your customers be glad they are doing business with your company if they were able to sit in on your sales meetings or watch them on closed circuit TV?

If you hesitate for even an instant to answer "yes" to each of those questions, we've got some work to do.

Let's consider each of these questions by themselves:

Would Your Salespeople Attend if Your Meetings Were Optional?

I hear sales managers talk all the time about *mandatory meetings* that likely take on a life of their own.

"We have a one-hour standing mandatory meeting, every Monday at 7:30 A.M.," said the new sales manager.

"Why?"

"Because we have always had a one-hour standing mandatory meeting."

Think about it this way: Each meeting you hold consumes both your salespeople's and your company's time and money.

Therefore, these meetings need to be purposeful and engaging. You have a meeting to get the ideas and opinions of those gathered—and to help them sell more efficiently in the coming week or month.

If a meeting doesn't tap into the group's knowledge—if you just want to pontificate for an hour—then please, just put it in writing and send it in an e-mail.

It's hard to impress the same salespeople week after week, sales meeting after sales meeting. When I was a sales manager, I had come up with 50 new meetings every year. That's tough work. Today, I blow into town, do my 75-minute keynote and catch a plane to the next city. While that's great for me, an hour and 15 minutes is usually not enough time to impart all of the skills the people in the audience need to develop.

At one point in my life, I thought I wanted to be a minister, a lawyer, a congressman, or a college professor. The common link among those careers is public speaking. I had no idea that there was such a thing as a professional speaker. So, I took a teaching course in college and prepared to *practice teach* my first class. I can remember it like it was yesterday, and it isn't a pretty picture. The people in the class dozed, read magazines, passed notes, talked amongst themselves, and basically ignored me for 50 minutes. Their body language screamed, "I dare you to try to teach me something." I now understand why tenured professors only teach a few classes and send the teaching assistants out to do the survey and 101 classes. When you are teaching someone who is fascinated by the subject, you have their full attention and participation. Otherwise, teaching is very tough.

This experience is still a vivid memory 36 years later. In the past 24 years, I have delivered more than 2,100 seminars and have never had an audience as tough as the one I faced in that small classroom back at Baldwin-Wallace College—because, you see, the course I was teaching was a *required* course. The worst audiences are often the ones that are *required* to be there.

So, what does this tell you? Perhaps, if you run a standing or required meeting every week, you might get the sense that people aren't fully engaged. If the meeting were *elective* or optional—would people come?

Jay Leonardi does instructional design for large companies and conducts seminars on various topics. With a master's degree in human resources, Jay served as a training director for a large insurance company and large bank before starting his own business. He explains,

> Most salespeople dread sales meetings because they waste their time and they don't get anything out of them. Too many sales managers position the meetings as reporting sessions and ask questions like:
>
> - What did you do?
> - Where did you do it?
> - What are the numbers?
>
> It ends up being de-motivating for anyone who missed their numbers, because they receive immediate—and public—negative consequences. Another thing managers may do poorly is make their meetings all about presentation and one-way information. He or she will say, "Okay, here's the new product information"—and then drone on for five or ten minutes while the salespeople sit there and think about how they should be out on the street making sales. At the end, the sales manager says, "What questions do you have?" And he's greeted with dead silence, because he established an environment of one-way communication.
>
> Leaders of effective meetings need to set a less formal tone through which they encourage interaction among participants.

There need to be questions and answers going back and forth between meeting attendees. It's more of a conversation in which salespeople are asked to contribute and answer questions like:

- What ideas do you have?
- What mistakes have we made?
- What are you seeing in the field?

Not only do managers do too much lecturing; they lecture on the wrong topic. In my Leading Effective Sales Meetings course, I give participants a list of 90 sales meeting topics and ask them to identify the top ten most important topics for their next sales meeting. I inevitably receive feedback like, "I never thought about talking about those kinds of things in my meeting." The topics run the gamut from the week's big news to the amount of churn that we have. It might mean that we take time to look at changes that have occurred in the marketplace. We could review industry updates, lead generation sources, referral channels that salespeople may have discovered that they can share among themselves. We could discuss a competitor's new offering and the advantages we have over them. These are the kind of real-world topics salespeople can get behind and engage with.

Compare that kind of discussion with what your salespeople tend to hear over and over again: "We missed our numbers. You're killing me." After about a month of that, [it's no wonder that your] salespeople have lost interest. And whether they go elsewhere or quit without bothering to resign, the sales manager is partly to blame for the turnover—or at the very least, a highly unenthused group of salespeople.

Number one: Your sales meeting has to be agenda driven. Sales managers often think, "I'm just going to wing this." And since many sales managers are good speakers, they think they can get away with it. The agenda should have the items

numbered with a specific time allotted to each. I like to identify what the purpose of the agenda item is: Is it an update?
Is it an item that requires discussion? Who owns that
agenda item? Your salespeople need to know these things in
advance.

It's important to give meeting attendees roles. You might
say, "John, this week I want you to lead the discussion about
our competitor's new product." Giving out those mini-
assignments ahead of time and building them into the agenda
makes people feel they have a role in this, and they are not
just little sponges. This also gives the report more credibility
because it came [as a result of everyone's input—not just the
managers'].

Meetings are successful when salespeople leave with the
tools, knowledge, and motivation to achieve the sales results
you require. If your sales meeting degenerates into nothing
more than a series of reports and lectures about performance,
you might as well cancel the meeting. You have to be working
on skills and attitudes.

Finally, [you always want to] talk *with* the group, not at
them. Salespeople who have been promoted from the ranks
are usually a little tenuous about their own leadership, and
want to somehow be "in charge" of the meeting. They would
be much better off not trying to position themselves as the
smartest people in the room. You can even [take the approach
of] breaking people up into small groups and posing a question
to them. The sales manager can capture the ideas on a flip
chart. Putting people in groups makes them feel somewhat
more obligated to contribute and produce a work product. You
become a meeting facilitator instead of a meeting chair.
Remember: "You are there to guide instead of tell."

If you're a leader and you're not letting others lead at least
part of the meeting, I wonder if you sometimes feel like I did
the first time I tried to be the teacher.

Would They Gladly Pay Five Dollars per Hour to Attend?

This is a profound question. If your salespeople are not getting a result or a return on investment (ROI) from attending your meetings, they may find them de-motivating—or, at worst, a waste of time. Donald Kirkpatrick is the founder of the American Society of Training and Development. Many years ago, he sent shock waves through the HR community by suggesting that trainers should try to document the ROI of their training.

Very few trainers want to be held accountable for ROI because they have a difficult time proving that what they do translates into real income for the company. But if you are running a meeting and working a little sales training in at the same time, it's a good idea to keep in mind Kirkpatrick's five levels of evaluating the meeting or training session.

Level 1—Reactions. You can ask your people to rate your sales meeting on a 1–10 scale for a variety of criteria:

- Did the meeting start and end on time?
- Was there an agenda?
- Did the information help me do my job better?
- Was this a good use of my time?
- Did I learn something new or get a new way to think about something old?
- If I had paid five dollars to attend this meeting, could I get at least a tenfold return on that investment?

Notice that I didn't mention anything about liking or disliking the meeting. You're there for their improvement, not their enjoyment. While learning *can* be enjoyable, you want people to evaluate the meeting using criteria that gives them a chance to rate their experience—and you want to use their feedback to get better. Think of your salespeople as your primary customers. Just like a restaurant or an online company that wants to know what you thought of the experience, you can find out how your sales meetings are coming across to those in attendance.

Level 2—Learning. The second level of evaluating a meeting or training session, according to Kirkpatrick, is learning. Did your salespeople get new information that they didn't have before attending the meeting? And keep in mind that knowing isn't doing. You can give people a pop quiz at the end of your meeting to see if they learned what you wanted them to or you can debrief a salesperson during one-on-one meeting to see what she took from your meeting. But knowing something isn't the same as doing something. That happens in . . .

Level 3—Transfer. Transfer of learning means that the behavior you were discussing actually made its way into the field. A salesperson tried a new approach or asked a new closing question. Only then can you get to . . .

Level 4—Results. A result can be positive or negative. You tried a different prospecting approach and you got the first meeting, or you got shot down. This is why *transfer* is the most important aspect to measure—because until people *do* something with what they learned, they cannot get a result for you to coach. And without transfer to the field, there will never be . . .

Level 5—ROI. You taught salespeople a new skill or rolled out a new initiative. Your salespeople transferred a new skill or presented the new initiative in front of a customer and got a result, an order in this case. You got a return on your investment for the meeting or training session.

Bottom line: If you focus only on imparting knowledge and skills without coaching to make sure your people actually did something, you have only done half of the job.

Would Your Customers Be Glad They Are Doing Business with Your Company If They Were Able to Sit in on Your Sales Meetings or Watch Them on Closed Circuit TV?

Are you asking your salespeople to say something about your product or service that you wouldn't want your customers to know? If your customers sat in on the meeting, would they feel that you have their best interests in mind and that you truly want to help them succeed? Would having a customer at your meeting create positive word of mouth for your company and referrals to other people in that customer's network—or not?

I like to think I have never done a sales meeting or a sales seminar that I would be ashamed or afraid to have a customer attend. What about you?

Here's another way to look at this same issue: What would you do differently in your sales meetings if a customer were there? Now, use that answer to plan your sales meeting as if your biggest customer were going to be in the room. Repeat weekly.

To Get Faster Results from Your Training Initiative Slow Things Down

I can relate to the following quote from E.B. White: "I get up every morning determined to both change the world and have one hell of a good time. Sometimes this makes planning my day difficult."

Actually, I'm only trying to change the sales training world. And even that is not easy. Maybe you can help me. You see, if I can change the way executives *think* about and sign off on training, then I can at least change their world for the better. The problems, as we've covered before, tend to be as follows:

- Most executives think of sales training as an *event* instead of a *process*.
- Too many of them buy training by the *hour* instead of the *outcome*.
- And most trainers and training departments think in terms of *courses and programs* instead of *knowledge bites* and *just-in-time information*.

Don't get me wrong; I still love to speak at annual sales meetings and conduct the occasional seminar. I just can't teach an audience everything I know in three hours. And most audience members come to a conference hoping to get *one good idea* anyway.

Earlier, I related the story about going to a weekend-long golf school and being overwhelmed by taking too many lessons in too short a time. My buddy Larry admonished me to slow down and take a short lesson to focus on one thing. I not only took that to heart, I changed much of the business model based on Larry's insight because it so obviously applies to sales and sales management training, too.

My current obsession is creating short, digestible *knowledge bites* and putting them online where salespeople can access and learn from them 24/7.

A salesperson who has left 25 voice mail messages with no calls returned can download a four-minute knowledge bite on voice mail scripting and apply the learning a few minutes later. That saves companies time and money. Plus, it is much better to put the learning in the field closer to the customers and prospects. And by working on just one thing that he really needs to work on, a salesperson will be more motivated to learn.

Each week, I create a new knowledge bite. I write, record, and upload them weekly to a web site called *Fuel*. I also put together an *Instant Sales Meeting* slideshow and four to six discussion questions.

This lets my customers run what I call "The Honors Class in Selling" sales meeting. It's an honors class because your salespeople actually listen to the knowledge bite three to five days ahead of the meeting. They can even implement an idea in the field and come back to the meeting to discuss what happened.

Because the knowledge bites run from two to seven minutes, they are "digestible."

There is a fee for this, but because you are reading this book, I will activate a one-month trial membership for you so you can run at least two meetings my way and see for yourself how much more effective this kind of ongoing, time-released sales training is.

Each week, you will get better at letting your salespeople take responsibility for their own development instead of trying to train them and tell them how to get better.

Your salespeople are coming to the meeting prepared to discuss the lesson. You don't have to worry about holding an engaging sales meeting; since they should be arriving with opinions and stories to share, they will do most of the heavy lifting. The best sales meetings are the ones that stimulate highly participative discussions of real-world issues.

There is a better way. I invented it. My customers swear by it. You can try it by e-mailing me at chris.lytle@sparque.biz.

The Meeting after the Sales Meeting

Whether we like to admit it or not, there is often a meeting after the sales meeting. It is held at the watercooler or the coffee shop around the corner shortly after the official sales meeting has ended. It's where salespeople *debrief and discuss* the content of the meeting they just attended.

This *meeting after the meeting* phenomenon occurs because salespeople often don't get to participate fully in the *real* sales meeting. The sales manager has imparted wisdom, but hasn't taken the time to get everyone involved.

There are times when one-way communication is necessary. However, if you are conducting sales training or trying to get buy in, it is absolutely crucial to get everyone involved.

I suggest running one of the aforementioned "Honors Class in Selling" sales meetings for your learning sessions. I took this idea from Dr. Murray Sperber's book *Beer and Circus: How Big-time College Sports Is Crippling Undergraduate Education*, in which he writes:

> After sitting in on an honors class at a Big-time U, a high school senior on a college visiting tour explained, "They spent the hour [discussing] the professor's specialty. The kids had done all the required reading and even the supplementary stuff. They asked the professor constant questions, interrupted him, argued all the time with him and each other. It must be so hard for profs to teach them."
>
> The interviewer replied, "No, it's like teaching graduate students. Most faculty members could roll out of bed at 3 A.M. and do it. But try teaching regular undergraduates who haven't done the reading and won't say a thing. Now *that's* hard teaching—straight uphill." Regular undergraduates can also crush faculty egos, whereas honors students flatter the professorial psyche and give faculty the illusion of being great

teachers (some educators term honors students *pre-learners*, in other words, they master most things on their own, with no need of formal instruction.)

What if your weekly sales meeting were this kind of an *honors class?* You could let salespeople master the topics on their own and debate and discuss the content they had learned before the session. By having everyone participate fully, there would be no need for your reps to run the meeting after the meeting at the coffee shop around the corner—since they've already debriefed and discussed the content of the sales meeting *at the sales meeting.*

Do you believe your salespeople are capable of participating in their own learning? What if your sales meetings were so engaging that there was no need for a post-meeting meeting?

Now we're talking.

Self Development and Homework

Remember, only 10 percent of your salespeople have a learning mindset. Unless it is part of a job requirement, don't expect them to pick up a book or subscribe to a trade publication that might help them succeed on the job.

No, if learning is going to be part of your competitive go-to-market strategy, you will have to manage and monitor it.

Leaders are readers. Heck, forget reading! These days, you can download podcasts, books, and jump on YouTube to see what's out there. You can attend college lectures on business or simply read the *Wall Street Journal.* But you have to set the tone and demand that your salespeople complete some sort of *homework* and personal research. Whether it's a chapter a week in a business best seller or a three-minute knowledge bite from a web site, you have to manage their learning or it will never happen in 90 percent of the cases.

The Best Sales Meetings Get People Involved

As the years go by, many sales managers develop a routine that causes their sales meetings to become numbingly boring and predictable. There is certainly nothing wrong with ritual and routine. However, when salespeople know exactly what's coming, they are more likely—and able—to tune in and out of the proceedings.

Keep them off guard. Don't get in a rut yourself. With that in mind, here are . . .

Twenty-Three Ways to Add Impact, Variety, and Even Suspense to Keep Your Salespeople Engaged

You want salespeople to be more knowledgeable and committed at the end of the meeting than they were when they walked into it. To that end, I've designed the following checklist to inspire you to change up your routine a bit—to do something different to keep your team engaged and maybe even a little off balance:

1. **Invite a guest speaker.** Some possibilities include:
   - Your CEO, president, VP of marketing, or plant manager; after all, these are some of the people who know your company best.
   - A local college football coach always has a good 30-minute motivational talk that will usually lead to a lively follow-up discussion.
   - A business professor from the local or community college could brief your team on the current economic

conditions or lecture on business principles. Being able to *talk business* instead of simply talking features, benefits, and pricing will make the members of your sales force more of a resource to your customers. They become known for what they **know** and not just what they sell.

- Let a satisfied customer brief your team. That meeting will build belief in your salespeople. Ask the buyer to take them through the buying process her team went through to make the purchase. She can highlight what went well and what needs to be improved. And finish by focusing on the results and ROI the buyer's company realized by implementing your solution.

- Bring in a sales manager from another unit of your own company to lead the meeting, or ask a sales manager from another company to speak to your team for about 30 to 45 minutes. Ask any guest sales manager to talk about the best practices that their teams use. Of course, they can reprise their very best sales meeting content for their one-time appearance.

2. **Use video**. You can do this in a number of ways:

- Look into renting a sales training video, or some material on business etiquette.

- Google hundreds of available titles at Biz Library or Mind Perks, and see which ones might benefit your employees. There is even a book devoted to business lessons from the movie *Movies for Leaders: Management Lessons from Four All-Time Great Films*. (For more information on this, visit www.moviesforbusiness .com.)

- Go to YouTube and search under terms like *motivation, sales speeches, sales training, business lecture, college course business*, and see what happens. Now *that's* content!

- You can find clips on YouTube of the following movies that feature salespeople in action. Of course, you can rent or download them, too:
  - *The Big Kahuna*
  - *Boiler Room*
  - *Glengarry Glen Ross*
  - *Jerry Maguire*
  - *Diamond Men*
  - *Tommy Boy*
  - *Death of a Salesman*
  - *Tin Men*
  - *City Slickers*
  - _____ (insert your favorite here).
- Set aside a longer session to watch a classic like *The Music Man* and hold a discussion about what Professor Harold Hill does right and wrong as he sells band instruments in River City, Iowa.

3. **Have a *facts frenzy* meeting.**

- Require salespeople to bring in customer trade publications and/or search business web sites to obtain articles and editorials from industry magazines and newspapers.
- Go through the articles for 45 minutes to an hour to find relevant articles to clip and send to prospects and customers. This exercise and practice is another way you become known for what you *know*—not just what you sell.

4. **Move the meeting off-site.**

- Ask a customer or local business to let you meet in their conference room or boardroom.

- Meet at your bank's conference room or boardroom.
- Go to a local university and meet in a classroom. (This, of course, is a good place to have a professor be your guest lecturer.)

The following can serve as your *cheat sheet* for leading a discussion after a hosting guest speaker, watching a video, listening to audio, reading an article, or taking a field trip. Ask one of these questions, and then let the salespeople carry the discussion.

- What one or two key points did you take from the presentation?
- How do these apply to you directly?
- What can you specifically do about this information?
- To which particular customer or prospect can you apply what you've learned?
- What might be the consequences of implementing this idea?
- What other support or training do you need in order to be confident in applying this idea?
- When will you take that action?

I suggest you do this as a *whip-around*—a training term that refers to an instructional strategy that's designed to get input from everyone at the table or in the room. You pose a question, and then give everyone a minute or two to think. Once someone volunteers an answer, go right around the table in one direction getting input from all of the others. You can allow some people to pass, but try to get as much participation as possible.

5. **Conduct a Mastermind session**. Ask your salespeople to come to the meeting with a problem or issue, and get a solution from the group instead of the sales manager.

This requires trust and openness, and can do wonders to build teamwork and shorten the learning curve. You want to foster a climate in which salespeople have to be willing to *raise their hands and ask for help.*

6. **Attend a live local presentation as a team**. Pick a seminar or lecture and go. The presentation can be one of those traveling leadership/motivation/business/sales seminars that fill an arena or an appearance of a local author at a bookstore. You might even take them to see a candidate stumping for office—the ultimate sales job—and even record the stump speech to see how the candidate tailored it to the town or the situation in which he found himself. Many times, a local business journal will sponsor a symposium or economic summit. These can be two-hour breakfast or luncheon meetings where you also have the opportunity to network. The message you send to your team is that stopping to learn occasionally will make us more effective in front of customers.

7. **Hold a debate**. Select two teams, give them a topic a week in advance, and ask each team to be able to argue both the pros and cons of the subject. Debates make salespeople—and really, everyone—look at both sides of the issue and be able to argue either side. They foster preparation as well as listening and thinking on one's feet. Some suggested debate topics:

- Resolved: We should lower the price we charge to customers.
- Resolved: We should raise the price we charge to customers.
- Resolved: We should charge for the consultation we do before we make a sale.

- Resolved: We should not respond to requests for proposals (RFPs) that we didn't know are coming.

8. **Give a pop quiz.** See what your salespeople know about current events, your products and services, the people in your company, and your competition. I can almost guarantee that they don't know everything they need to know. Trade papers, and have them grade each other's work. Announce the winner and runner up, and award a prize to the winner.

   Salespeople need to be up-to-date on current events to be able to make small talk with potential customers—something that builds rapport. Give your team members a quiz about local business, politics, and sports to see how aware they are about current events. You can also quiz them on the following topics:

   - Their product knowledge on both new and old products and services
   - The history of the company
   - The competition
   - The information they should have learned at the last training session or sales meeting

9. **Hold a practice session and incorporate video feedback.**

   - Use a sales meeting to practice the first three minutes of the most important presentation your salespeople have coming up in the next couple of weeks.
   - Have someone record them while they practice the last two pages of it, including the close.
   - Watch the video with the person practicing. Have him point out three things he likes, and one thing he wants to improve in his approach.
   - Let other observers identify three things the salesperson did well and one thing to make better.

10. **Assign a book report.**
    - Have your salespeople read a book or a chapter of a book that you choose, or take suggestions from the group.
    - Ask everyone to report on one or two key usable points they extracted from the reading.

11. **Use a learning game or experiential exercise.** Experiential learning gets salespeople to participate in an exercise or simulation, discuss what they learned, and then apply the lessons to their everyday tasks. Unless you tie the experience to the job, you are just playing games and taking up time. A few I use are:
    - *Games Trainers Play* (McGraw-Hill Training Series)—Paperback (May 1, 1980), by Edward Scannell and John Newstrom
    - *More Games Trainers Play*
    - *Even More Games Trainers Play*
    - *Sales: Games and Activities for Trainers*—Paperback (May 1, 1997) by Gary Connor and John Woods
    - *Games That Drive Change*—Paperback (July 1, 1995) by Carolyn Nilson

12. **Conduct a *brag* or storytelling session.** Ask one of your salespeople to walk the group through a successful and significant sale she has made. She should talk in detail about the sale—from the moment she got the lead until she landed the order. After the story, conduct a discussion about what went well and what roadblocks had to be overcome.

13. **Schedule Field Trips.** Some potential destinations:
    - Go to a library and read sales books for an hour; then spend another hour discussing what you learned.

- Visit a customer facility. Get a guided tour to see the space through the customer's eyes.
- Go to your own production facility and receive a briefing from the people who actually *make* your products.
- Check out an exhibit at a local museum or art gallery to get people to observe something completely outside of their current viewpoints.
- Attend a local sports team practice to watch how a coach teaches the fundamentals. Hold a discussion of sales fundamentals and what needs work in a salesperson's basic set of skills.
- Meet for breakfast early one day, and hold your business meeting shortly after that.
- Take your team to a fine dining restaurant, and encourage them to observe the kind of service they receive. Afterward, talk about the experience you had from the greeting through ordering your meal, to paying the bill and the good-bye at the end. Discuss your experience as customers in detail, and apply your observations to how you might treat your customers better or differently based on the meal you had.

14. **Prospect for an hour.** Gary Buchanan, president of Three Eagles Broadcasting, has a wonderful approach he uses in situations like these. When he visits one of the company's markets, he takes the sales team on a field trip in a large passenger van. They get some fast food, and armed with legal pads, the CEO drives them around town yelling out names of businesses on every street and asking who is calling on them.

    "What I find is we drive up and down the same roads every day to see a customer and fail to pay attention. In most cases our salespeople come home with a long list of new prospects to see."

As you might imagine, it teaches a valuable lesson on the importance of prospecting if the president of the company is that interested in it. Whether you rent a van or search the Internet for new prospects, there is something to be said about using the sales meeting to actively prospect instead of talking about the need to prospect.

15. **Change the room set up**. Though it sounds simple, even doing something as basic as setting the room differently can alter a meeting's sense of staleness and predictability. Use a round table and, instead of standing at the head of a conference table, sit with the team and let *them* carry the discussion.

16. **Hold a *standing* brainstorming session (instead of sitting around a table)**.

   - Bring in flip charts or whiteboards and pose a question. Set aside seven minutes to come up with, say, 10 things that make your company a better choice than Competitor A for a customer.
   - Focus on the quantity of ideas first; this will elicit more ideas and makes people think past the obvious first few ideas. The time limit keeps them focused. Have the flip chart be the focus of the meeting, and make sure that everyone is standing around it. This creates a different dynamic and energy than sitting around a conference table.
   - Set up several flip charts and position groups of three to five people around them; this will trigger a sense of competition and bring forth even more ideas.
   - Have everyone report on their lists, and then discuss the best 7 to 10 ideas. This will keep everyone thinking

about the issue and gaining product knowledge long after the meeting is over.

17. **Use the sales meeting to get something done instead of learn something.**

    • Write three thank-you notes or notes of appreciation to customers, people who've referred you to others, past speakers—anyone who deserves recognition.

    • Plan the most important meeting you have that week with a coach. Work in pairs. One rep asks pre-meeting planning questions. The other rep answers.

    • Have your salespeople do some pre-meeting research on a customer or category of customer, and spend the meeting discussing what everyone's learned.

18. **Discuss news articles.**

    • Pass out an article from a trade publication or web site and discuss the implications of the article for your sales force and their customers.

    • Create an action plan for bringing the article to the attention of more prospects and customers.

19. **Practice memorization techniques.** Use the meeting to devise answers to the most commonly heard customer objections or concerns, and have your salespeople work on memorizing the answers. Salespeople should leave the sales meeting with a written answer and have practiced the answer at least seven times during the session.

20. **Engage in action planning.**

    • Ask salespeople what they are going to do with new learning, and have them submit a detailed action plan on it. The plan should outline the behavior they are going to implement, the prospect or customer with whom they will try the new behavior, and the date by which they will do it.

- Get a copy of the person's action plan. I assume you have a tickler system—a set of file folders where you file papers for the date on which you may want to look at them. I would file the salesperson's action plan in the tickler file for one or two weeks from now. Or, simply file it in the file you keep for each of your salespeople. And when you sit down for your one-on-one meeting, grab the action plan and find out what happened with that particular situation. Make sure to praise the salesperson for trying a new behavior, and coach him along by asking what went well, and what he might do differently next time to achieve even better results. Here's how that might go:

  - "John, you stated in your action plan that you would use the pre-meeting assignment with Mr. Barnes at the ABC Company."

    Then continue asking questions:

  - Have you done that yet?
  - What results did you experience?
  - How did it feel using this skill with that prospect?
  - How did he react?
  - What would you do differently if you could rewind and do it over?
  - Have you used it with anyone else?
  - How will you use and modify this new skill going forward?

Remember: You're coaching, not training. And the secret of coaching is to draw people out—and not pour your ideas in. Again, the *rule* here is to ask those all-important seven questions before you give an answer.

The fact that you remember to inspect and hold people accountable to their action plans will make learning part of your culture over time. You want to hear exchanges around the office like, "Dude, when you say you are going to do something, the manager remembers and calls you on it."

21. **Send out a meeting agenda two to three days in advance with the sales meeting objective.** Give the salesperson a pre-meeting assignment—something to read, watch, listen to, or do before the sales meeting. This action becomes each person's *ticket to the sales meeting.*

22. **Nominal group process.** In small groups of three to five people, ask salespeople to discuss a topic and come to some conclusions.

    - Report those conclusions to other groups
    - Note the differences in the reports
    - Create a list of ideas for action from all of the groups

23. **Meet via Web tools such as *Go to Meeting, Go to Webinar,* or *WebEx*.** Hold a meeting where salespeople share winning proposals, successful interactions with customers, or a letter or voice mail script that landed a first meeting.

    - Share desktops and documents for others to use
    - Identify best practices from things that are currently working

    Bonus meeting: One of my *imbedded* salespeople remembers a sales meeting where the company's owner spent an hour having his salespeople walk up to him and shake hands. The day before this meeting, a salesperson calling on the owner had made a horrible impression with a wet fish handshake. The owner couldn't stand the thought of his salespeople making the same mistake on their own prospects.

How to End Any Meeting

I learned a very powerful lesson on one of my winter vacations that has changed the way I end my meetings.

We were in Bermuda—my wife Sarah, her brother Bob, and his wife Kathy. Our condo was in St. George at one tip of the island. At about 9:00 A.M., we boarded our motor scooters to drive to breakfast. Then, we headed to Hamilton (the big city) to sightsee, shop, and have lunch. At 2:00 P.M., we arrived at the golf course and played 18 holes.

This takes us to cocktail hour, where we watched the sun set over the ocean and partook in one of mine and Sarah's favorite vacation rituals: to ask each other, "What was the highlight of your day?"

"So, what was the highlight of your day?" I asked.

"I'll start," said Kathy. "It was when we turned the corner on the North Road and I saw the pink sand beaches. I know the guidebook said they would be there, but it was stunning to see it with my own eyes. I'll never forget it."

"Bob?" I said.

"For me, it was when we passed the airport on the way to breakfast. Remember the plane that was sitting there with its wings folded up? I don't think the general public is supposed to be seeing those. That was a special airplane and it's amazing that we got that close."

Sarah went next. "I would have to say it was the lunch in Hamilton. I've always loved that little balcony restaurant where we ate. But today, the temperature was so nice, and the harbor was the perfect blue. And that made the food even more enjoyable."

Finally, it was my turn. "Didn't anyone see me save par from the sand on the 17th hole? That was definitely the highlight for me."

We finished our drinks and moved on to dinner, but the conversation stayed with me—and here's why: The four of us took two motor scooters to the same breakfast place, shopped at the same stores, ate at the same lunch place, played at the same golf course, and were sitting on the same patio debriefing our day. We essentially all had *the same day*! But everyone had a unique highlight, and processed the *experience* of that same day differently.

At the end of your sales meetings, you want to ask each of your salespeople: "What was the highlight of this meeting for you?" You cannot assume that they are taking away what you want them to take away unless you ask. They all attended the same meeting—but they processed the experience differently. You will also find this is a great way to review the entire meeting quickly and reinforce the key points.

You want your salespeople to ask their prospects and customers the same question after their meetings. "What was the highlight of this meeting for you?" Or, "What are you taking away from this meeting that added value?" Ultimately, it doesn't matter what your salespeople thought about the meeting; what really matters is what the person across the desk from them thought about the meeting.

I don't think you can overuse this question with anyone— your spouse, children, sales team, or customers. You already know what *you* think. What you need to find out is what *other* people think.

What Happens in Your Meeting in Vegas Stays in the Meeting Room

The Wake-Up Call

There was a particular TV commercial that opened with a hotel guest calling the front desk to ask for an 8:30 A.M. wake-up call. But he wonders if it would be possible to direct that wake-up call to his cell phone instead of the phone in his room. You see, he's in Las Vegas and he's not sure exactly where he's going to be waking up the next morning. The commercial ends with the now famously tawdry tag line:

"Las Vegas: What happens here stays here."

The Las Vegas Convention and Visitors Authority's annual ad budget is $115 million. The "What happens here, stays here" campaign is fueling controversy while filling the city's hotels, casinos, and convention halls with new and repeat revelers.

Las Vegas has abandoned its once family-friendly image to reclaim its "Sin City" heritage. There are high stakes in the Las Vegas meeting business, as *Selling Power* magazine reports, "the average budget for company sales meetings is $421,026. Nearly 24 percent have budgets of $1 million or more for the annual meeting."

Unfortunately, once you decide to hold the annual sales meeting in Las Vegas, the *house* has already won.

"Good Morning, it's 8:30 A.M."

Let's pretend that the guy from the Las Vegas commercial is one of your salespeople, in town to attend your firm's annual sales meeting. It's a nice perk after a tough year. Wherever his night may end, his morning begins with a successful wake-up call to his cell phone. Sleep-deprived and sorely in need of a breath mint, he arrives at the first session. He misses the Continental breakfast but grabs a cup of coffee and finds his place in the meeting room as the lights go down and the first speaker of the day approaches the podium.

As the professional speaker hired to address the Las Vegas sales meeting, I have looked into the vacant, bloodshot eyes of audience members who have spent the night before in Las Vegas and miraculously managed to make it to my 9:00 A.M. sessions. Sometimes I have looked only at their eyelids. I can confirm that "What happens here stays here" applies not only to whatever indiscretions they may have committed the night before; it also applies to the meeting and training content that the less-than-alert attendees are supposed to be internalizing. Most trainees leave Las Vegas—or any location where the annual meeting is held—without an action plan for implementing the new knowledge and skills you gathered them together to impart. Sadly, too many companies adopt a similar approach—and face a similar outcome: holding the training session, collecting the evaluations, and *then* beginning the planning for next year's session.

Case in point: The following is the text of an e-mail I received from one such attendee:

> Mr. Lytle, I would like to ask you to come to New Zealand and speak at our National Sales Conference at the end of January. We are looking at doing two really meaty sessions in one day: 10.30am–12.30pm & 3.00pm–6.00pm. I look forward to hearing from you. Joe R.

This, unfortunately, is typical of companies that make the mistake of buying training by the hour instead of by the outcome. Sure, it's flattering that someone in New Zealand has even heard of me. But flying anyone 35 hours to deliver five hours of training—meaty or otherwise—is a mistake unless there is going to be some kind of follow-up. Starting with hours instead of outcomes can be a mistake. Sales training is—or should be—a planned program that is designed to impart specific knowledge skills and attitudes to increase desired behavior in measurable ways.

The *outcome* ought to be stated as some measurable change in behavior that will gain a result for the company—increased sales, new accounts, or higher margin of business. The key to mounting a successful corporate education initiative is to ask questions about the outcomes you're seeking. This involves more than deciding on the duration of the session. Ask these five questions before you sign off on another conference, seminar, or corporate education initiative:

1. In behavioral terms, what would you like the audience members doing more or less of as a result of the meeting or training session?
2. How will this new behavior deliver a different outcome?
3. How will you measure it?
4. How will you reinforce and/or reward this new behavior?
5. What will be the consequences for those who choose not to change?

Companies that buy training by the hour instead of by the outcome perpetuate their problems and make expensive mistakes in the process. Business leaders endorse company get-togethers and feel the lift from such events that often bring everyone together—if only for a moment—to focus on the mission and perpetuate the culture. So far, so good. However, you can't confuse this kind of gathering with training. Training is measured by behavioral change that is beneficial to the company.

A Do-It-Yourself Annual Meeting Design

The plan below outlines a meeting that will get every one of your salespeople involved in a focused discussion. I suggest you devote at least 90 minutes to it, and let the discussion play out naturally. Nobody stands at the front of the room behind a podium; rather, the room is set with round tables that seat no more than five people and no less than three.

Purpose: To share your experiences and gain from others' experiences. Talking with your fellow salespeople can help you put your setbacks and successes in perspective, and sharing your experiences can help others.

Process: Working in small groups, you are going to have a conversation about selling in which you partake in the following:

- Sentence completion
- Answering questions posed by the group leader
- Responding to problems presented or questions asked of the group by an individual

Payoff:

- You will learn from people who do what you do every day
- You'll bring a problem and leave with a solution (or several)

- You will realize that we collectively know more about this business than any one individual knows, since all of us are smarter than one of us
- You will be able to tap into your peers' experiences

Instructions for the Group (Table) Leader: Your role is to pose a question and make sure everyone at the table has a chance to answer if he or she chooses. You also need to make sure that only one person is talking at any given time.

Instructions for Group Members: Your role is to contribute your own ideas, stories, and best practices as you answer the question. Please limit side conversations and listen to the person who is speaking. A good goal is to get three to five actionable ideas from people who do the same thing that you do.

The Three Segments of the Meeting

Sentence Completion (10 minutes): To get everyone off to a productive start, the group leader will ask members to complete the seven sentences below. When one person volunteers to answer a question, the person on his or her right answers next, and so on until you have gone around the table. Each person may pass, but only twice.

1. One thing I know for sure about succeeding in selling [product/company] is . . .
2. The one thing I learned about selling _____ the hard way is . . .
3. The best advice I ever got about selling from my manager is . . .

4. The best advice I ever got about selling from a customer is . . .

5. One thing I want to do more of in the upcoming quarter is . . .

6. One thing I am determined to do less of in the upcoming quarter is . . .

7. The best thing about being on the _____ sales team is . . .

Discussion Questions (45 Minutes to 1 Hour): Once you've warmed up with the sentence completions, the group leader can pose the following questions. We are looking for stories, examples, and specifics. Name names. Use numbers.

1. What *best practice* has helped you sell a major piece of business for our company?

2. What are you doing to grow your sales? (Describe as many or as few ideas as you are willing to share.)

3. What are you reading or studying to develop yourself?

4. How have other team members helped you facilitate a sale?

5. What is the biggest change you've seen in the business? How are you dealing with that change?

6. Did a failure or mistake you made teach you a great lesson? If so, what happened?

Ask a Question. Solve a Problem (15 to 30 Minutes): Is there a problem for which you would like feedback? Is there a question you would like to ask the group?

1. Give people three minutes to formulate their questions.
2. Let one person pose a question and solicit answers from group members.
3. Continue until all questions are asked and answered or until the time runs out.

As you can see from reading through this, you really don't have to do much more than ask the hotel to set up the room with round tables. The salespeople are the stars of this meeting. By getting everyone to share their experiences, it makes everyone feel less isolated and part of a bigger fraternity (or sorority) of people who have carried the bag. It lets people know they are not "home alone."

Home Alone (1990) is one of those movies that make me stop flipping through the channels and watch. It's a Christmas movie with spiders, cat burglars, a scary old man next door, and a cute little kid—and one of the highest grossing comedies of all time. So I guess I'm not the only one who likes it.

There is something about eight-year-old main character Kevin McCallister's determination to protect his home from the bumbling cat burglars that I find fascinating. Despite the fact that Kevin is deathly afraid of the basement furnace at the movie's beginning, he is bravely—and successfully—defending his turf by the end.

The sales and sales management lesson from *Home Alone* is that no child, or for our purposes, salesperson, should be left alone for very long.

You're Not *Home Alone*

Salespeople—heck anybody—can be a lot like Kevin McCallister. They may feel frightened and isolated on the job, and as though everyone is conspiring against them. They may feel their job—and security—is always on the line. Despite the fact that selling is a shared experience, it's one that your salespeople are having all by themselves. They may be *home alone* in their remote offices, or working their territory solo. It can be hard for them to review their day while sitting alone in a hotel room, or even at home at night with the family. After all, the daily grind of getting to the buyer is hardly the stuff of engaging dinner conversations; and the minutes or hours you spend with prospects and customers is rarely interesting to your spouse and kids.

Therefore, your job as manager is to get your salespeople to share, commiserate on, or celebrate these experiences—as the results warrant. One of the best reasons to have a sales meeting is to discuss what everyone has been going through—to hear and tell war stories. Knowing that you are not the only salesperson with doubts and worries is a first step. Hearing success stories from peers is more instructive than any seminar or book will ever be.

Peer pressure and peer successes are both good things.

When salespeople see other mere mortals accomplish what they're striving to achieve, they pick up on a powerful message: "If she can do it, I can do it. It *can* be done."

The do-it-yourself annual meeting creates the conversation that ends the feeling of isolation.

Five Factors that Foster Loyalty

Many company's use the annual meeting to award Chairman's Club or Quota Busters awards. And that's fine as far as it goes. In Chapter 3, I suggested you recognize members of your sales team every week. Remember?

An *Industry Week* survey isolated the following five factors for fostering loyalty. The comments after them are mine.

1. **Recognition:** 100 percent. People want to be part of a team solving real problems. Salespeople are *people* first. They need to be noticed.

2. **Challenging work:** 84.4 percent. People want challenging—not *overwhelming* work. I often spend an hour or two on a challenging crossword puzzle. Challenging work is stimulating, engaging, and fun.

3. **Increased pay:** 69.7 percent—*hmmm.*

4. **Dynamic boss:** 43.7 percent. Well, that should take some of the pressure off you.

5. **Years of service:** 40.7 percent. "I've worked here so long, I can't quit. I don't have any other marketable skills."

Though loyalty may seem like somewhat of a quaint concept, it would be nice if you got a little bit of loyalty from your salespeople—right? Of course, you can't *demand* loyalty; you must earn it. Loyalty starts from the top down, not the bottom up. And people become more loyal when they feel appreciated.

Sales Contests Are Usually a Bad Idea

There is a whole industry that creates sales incentives for salespeople. But how many flat-screen TVs or trips to the Australian Outback can you afford to hand out? And isn't this a form of manipulation? Do you want your salespeople working because they want to win something—or do you want them focused on your customer's needs and problems?

That said, the following are my four rules of running a sales contest that actually generates sales.

1. Everyone has to be able to win.
2. The contest should reinforce behavior and generate sales.
3. It should be short (13 weeks max, but probably less).
4. There must be consequences for not participating fully.

I believe the following contest does all of this—and quite effectively.

The Best Damn Sales Contest in the World: The 1,000 Yard Club

In the advertising business, the first two months of the year were nothing sales-wise compared to the run up that took place prior to Christmas. It is very easy for salespeople to slow down their own activity and rest up until spring. I can distinctly remember one particular management meeting which addressed this issue. How could we stimulate a flurry of activity starting the week between Christmas and the New Year that would continue into February? So we created something we called "The 1,000 Yard Club"—a contest in which salespeople had to *run* 1,000 yards over 10 weeks. They got weekly *yardage* by doing sales activities, which we doled out in the following way:

- 1 yard for targeting a specific account
- 3 yards for holding a first meeting with the account
- 5 yards for writing a *spec* commercial for a customer
- 5 yards for completing a needs analysis
- 10 yards for making a written presentation to the account
- 15 yards when the presentation included a sample ad
- 25 yards for closing a "Super Bowl" account

Lowell Yoder of M&T bank uses a similar theme, but instead of a football field, Yoder's is a NASCAR race track. Relationship managers earn *miles* by racing 500 miles in 10 weeks.

Whatever kind of contest or measures you choose, standards like these are measurable indicators of performance that involve consequences. If there are no standards, you have no discipline. The first step of sales management is to figure out what your people are already doing. The second is to give people the structure in which to succeed.

Account Decision Stress and Other Maladies

There are a couple of ideas I wanted to get across that don't warrant a whole chapter. But as you come to the end of this book, I wanted to share some ideas that are easy to implement and pay big dividends quickly.

Back when I first began my coaching career, the CEO of a new radio company called me with a dilemma. "My salespeople have account decision stress," is how he put it.

"Tell me about it," I said. I didn't admit that I had never heard of such a thing during my (then brief) career as a consultant.

"Well, we require them to make ten calls a day. So they head for a strip mall and do a lot of cold calling on the local retailers. The next day they go to another strip mall. After one week, they've make 50 calls, but there are literally hundreds maybe thousands of prospects in our suburban Chicago marketing area. So they can have 200 or 300 prospects on their lists."

I advised him, "Cut their lists down to 50 total accounts and make them call on the same 50 the next week. By the fourth week, they will have made 200 calls, but they will have seen 50 people four times."

"But then wouldn't we be leaving hundreds of customers untapped?"

"How many customers are writing you checks this month?"

"I'll have to get back to you on that."

"Best guess?"

"Less than 150."

"Then you don't need to be calling on 1,000 people. You have five salespeople; you need to be calling on 250. You need to do a great job of bringing ideas to them and showing them how to grow their businesses with your stations," I said. "When you're sending out 200 invoices a month, then you can add a sixth salesperson to call on 50 more accounts."

"I never thought of it that way," he admitted.

"If your salespeople know that they have to make their living on 50 accounts—and by the way, 35 would be better—then they won't have 'account decision stress.' They will have focus.

"Hold a meeting and tell them that you have just spent a fortune on a sales consultant who has advised you to give them some much-needed structure so they can maximize their efforts in the field. Let them keep any account who has written a check in the last six months. Then, put the rest of the accounts on one piece of paper and hold a draft. The last person who has made a sale gets the first pick, and so on until everyone has 50 accounts on their list. All of the other accounts are off limits. If someone that is not being called on contacts your company to request a salesperson, you can assign that account to the salesperson who has made the most recent sale.

"Tell your salespeople that they now have an account list—not a hunting license. Trying to sell and service hundreds of potential prospects will never lead to enough second and thirds calls to get the business."

He agreed, and I sent him a bill. His sales improved and I looked like a genius.

As a sales manager, it is your job to deploy people on the right prospects and the right number of prospects—or you *and* your employees will fail. It's also vital to realize that words matter—a lot. You set the tone early in your career by announcing that a salesperson is a steward of the company's accounts. Make it clear at the outset that this is the *company's* account list or territory—not the salesperson's. Use language like *our customers* and immediately correct a salesperson who uses phrases like *my customer* and *my account.* He may have brought this customer into the company, but it is the company's account. Remind him that if he is a good steward, he'll continue building a strong relationship with that account.

How to Double Your Sales without Doubling Your Efforts

What I'm about to share with you, I have taught to thousands of sales reps and watched as they discovered what it really means to work smarter instead of harder. All you have to do is teach it to your team and watch them succeed.

Let me guess. Your sales quota for next year is going to be more. Wall Street and the board members have one word that they like to use a lot: *more.* Sales managers are under the gun to get salespeople to sell more. So they immediately think in terms of *more calls, more proposals,* and *more activity.* And there is nothing wrong with that. At the same time, it is important to understand that salespeople already think they are giving their all. They're not; but they think they are.

If you are a VP of a billion dollar company who is reading this, you will have to add some zeroes to my numbers. But I wanted to keep this very simple and show you how quickly you can increase billing by doing a little—not a lot—more.

Part of your job is to help salespeople buy in to the new number instead of push back. Most quotas are incremental— 10 or 15 percent more than last year. Before you introduce that number, you want to have the conversation about doubling their sales.

Walk them through examples like the ones I am going to show you, but do it with their actual (there's that word again) numbers.

In this example, I look at two metrics: (1) the number of customers who wrote a check this month, quarter or year depending on your sales cycle, and (2) the average size of that check.

If you only concentrate on getting more customers without getting bigger checks from existing customers, you will have a hard time doubling your business.

What you are trying to do as per Figure 6.1 is to double your business by going from 20 to 40 customers without increasing the average dollars per customer. In the example displayed in Figure 6.2, I have taken the starting number at 20 billing accounts; you can insert your own number here. I have then increased the number of customers by 5 percent per month and the average dollar per customer by 10 percent per month.

Month	1	2	3	4	5	6	7
# Customers	20	24	28	30	32	36	40
Avg $	1,000	1,000	1,000	1,000	1,000	1,000	1,000
Billing	20,000	24,000	28,000	30,000	32,000	36,000	40,000

Figure 6.1   The "Hard Way" to Double Your Sales

Month	1	2	3	4	5	6	7
# Customers	20	21	22	23	24	25	26
Avg $	1,000	1,100	1,200	1,300	1,400	1,500	1,600
Billing	20,000	23,100	26,400	29,900	33,600	37,500	41,600

Figure 6.2   The "Easy Way" to Double Your Sales

And look what happens. In six months, **you have doubled sales**. But your haven't doubled the work.

Can—and will—your salespeople actually do this? Beats me. But it is more likely to happen if you focus on two metrics instead of one. If new business is simply combing the bushes for new customers, your salespeople will have a tough slog. But if they systematically sell to 5 percent more customers and up-sell current customers 10 percent a month, you will achieve staggering growth. I guarantee that if you don't pay attention to both numbers, you will be screaming "more" for the rest of your life.

I once heard sales trainer and author Mahan Khalsa claim in a speech that most managers have two buttons that they push: (1) the *more* button and (2) the *panic* button. And yet, what they need to be able to push is the *how* button.

Showing salespeople *how* they can sell more—a lot more— without working much harder is something few sales managers ever manage to do.

But not you—you have the magic of math at your disposal. Use it.

And after you have shown them how to double their billing, when you ask them for a 15 percent sales increase, they will be more likely to believe they can actually do it.

Reality Check: It's Not a "Great Meeting" unless the Customer Thinks It Was a Great Meeting

Whether you are having an annual meeting in Las Vegas, or a sales meeting in Bismarck, ND, the person chairing the meeting is not the one to declare it a "great meeting." That job falls to the audience members.

This also applies to a meeting a salesperson is having with a customer.

Though you and your salespeople may not realize it, your customers will more or less *tell* you how to sell to them. Asking questions—and really listening to the answers—is the solution to most sales problems. If you ask the right questions—and ask them early on—your customers will guide you through the process.

Unfortunately, too many salespeople believe that they already have to have the answers and solutions. Make no mistake: There is a lot to be said for pre-meeting preparation; it's good to know a few things about the prospect's business. Yet at the same time, it is very important to understand what's going on *right now* in the prospect's operation.

If you think about it, the customer's agreeing to meet with you is a buying signal. The **first meeting** is an opportunity to start—or end—a relationship. Salespeople who pitch first and ask questions later usually find themselves asking the question, "Why didn't I get an order or a second meeting?"

See if you agree with this statement: When a prospect agrees to a meeting, something has happened. I refer to it as a *triggering event*—something that took place either internally or externally to get the person to consider your offering. It might be a problem with a current supplier, or a competitive threat from the outside. But there is always something going on that prompts new purchases or changes.

Here are three good questions you can ask a prospect early in the meeting. Listening to the answers will get the customer to tell you the real problem, and will allow you to tailor your presentation and solution.

1. **Why did you agree to a meeting today instead of three months ago?**

This can give the client information about the triggering event.

2. **"At the end of our conversation, what will have had to happen for you say it was a good meeting?"**

If you let the customer think about and answer that question, you will know exactly what to present and what *not* to present. It can also get the customer to reveal the problems or opportunities in his business. Finding out what the customer wants out of the meeting—and knowing what he thinks "good" looks like—allows you to align your behavior and your presentation.

3. **"What do you already know about our company so I don't bore you with my voluminous product knowledge?" Or, "What would you like to know about our company that you don't know already?"**

I like to think I'm a decent sales trainer. But if you ask, your customer will do an even better job than I can in guiding you through the sales process.

The Courtesy Call

I went to a seminar when I was a new sales manager where the speaker claimed that as a sales manager, you ought to call up every customer once a quarter, identify yourself and your company, and ask the following question:

"What can we do to provide you with better service?"

So I started doing it. And I learned a lot about my sales team and their professionalism—or lack thereof, in certain instances. This habit also kept me connected to the customer in situations of salesperson turnover. And it gave me plenty of sales meeting fodder.

The more you do something like this, the more your prospects and customers will expect it. The longer you keep up the habit, the better the answers you will get because your prospects and customers know you are going to be calling.

So ask them: "What could we do to provide you with better service?" And truly listen to the response. Your customer will tell you things that will help you coach your team better and give you insight into how your people are really doing in the field.

I passed this idea along to many sales managers over the years, one of whom was Mike Varney. Mike called a customer and asked the question, and received the following reply.

"In order to provide me better service, you would have to get a salesperson from your company to call on me," said the customer.

It turns out the salesperson wasn't making the calls he reported.

It might be nice to know a little thing like that, too.

Every salesperson that is actually doing his or her job will be *glad* you are calling the customer. It shows that someone else at the company cares about the customer's experience. And what salesperson wouldn't want to get helpful advice on how to keep the customer happy?

Your marketing department could spend two weeks creating a survey and sending an e-mail to every customer hoping to get a 15 percent response rate. Then, they will take 30 more days to slice and dice the data.

You will get more usable information by asking one question in real time of another human being.

Trust me on this one.

Of course, there are salespeople whom you can trust implicitly. I'm just wondering if you know exactly which ones.

Shrewd sales managers confirm salespeople were where they said they were. This is very important with new hires and middle of the road performers.

Your Legacy, or, Why Are You Doing This Besides the Money?

Was it worth it? In my conversations with sales managers, I wanted to find out the psychic rewards of leading a sales force.

Jim Lobaito says the following:

Sales management is truly a thankless job. Because you have your crazy boss who calls you in for a meeting and says, "Why can't we do this?" Whatever "this" is. You don't want to argue with him, but you say, "Well, because that's not realistic."

But you have your marching orders. And I would go back to my office and think, "That was kind of crazy, but we still have to get there." Then, I would translate what the boss wants into a language that my salespeople could understand and somehow make it happen.

You have a boss with unrealistic expectations and salespeople who think what you're asking them to do is unrealistic, too. So you're caught in the middle.

For years, I was fed by that. It is very challenging, but not everyone is fed that way. You have to be fed by the fact that you're willing to make a difference in the lives and the careers of the people underneath you.

Because they can't pay you enough to do the job.

The payment has to come from your desire to make a difference. In other words, those employees are better off for having worked for you than if they had worked somewhere else. Even the ones who don't make it.

So that was my philosophy. It kept me going for years. Because I truly felt and I got affirmation back from salespeople that their experience—whether it was a short time with us or a long tenure—was one of the best experiences in their career.

Michael Draman, VP of sales for Nexstar Broadcasting, claims, "You empower people by listening to them. It's all about being heard."

"In other words—people have to know that it's okay to mess up once in a while. They've got to know that you are going to be there for them regardless of their imperfections.

"Why do I do this? I've been a Marine. I've done Special Ops. I've had the testosterone rush. I've done the recon thing and jumped out of airplanes from ridiculous heights. It's not about that anymore. Now, it's really about teaching, and believing in a team. It's coming to places that—for lack of a better word—are viewed for one reason or another as broken, and fixing them. And the way to fix them is not by mending or changing the processes so much as making the *people* better. I enjoy doing that. I look around at all of the groups I've helped in the past, and I'm still very proud of what I helped them accomplish. They got it done because they were given the right support, the right coaching, and the appropriate discipline. Seeing somebody better today than they were a year ago is a very good feeling. That's an adrenalin rush. Your legacy as a professional is embodied in the kind of professionals—and people—that you leave behind."

For Windstream's Dave Snodgrass, it's seeing his team grow in both income and confidence:

I love to see people I have brought into a sales role [become] successful and make more money than they have ever made in their career. It's gratifying to see them rewarded for their hard work. They feel like they have accomplished something significant. They're happier. Their hard work has paid off. And the benefits trickle down to their spouses, families, and their charities. It's huge. Another thrill is seeing salespeople who've struggled gain confidence and direction. And finally, it's truly rewarding and fun when you help foster the relationship with key customers that develop into rewarding long-term connections—even after a rep has left the company.

Continues Snodgrass:

"I have been part of once-small companies that have experienced significant growth. Getting to see salespeople learn and grow from that—and experience that ride when two or three years go by so quickly—is an amazing thing. It's about the things you learned and experiences you've had and income you achieved and sacrifices you made along the way. Those situations provide you with a window—a short period of time to catch that wave and ride it, which is a wonderful experience. You know the wave doesn't go on forever, so you have to enjoy it."

Gary Miles looks at his legacy in a similar fashion: "The best satisfaction was seeing people who entered our organization and ended up becoming general managers, sales managers, and program directors. The next one is to see the evolution of these people as they advance and move on to more successful jobs. It is the thing that is the most satisfying."

Phil Fisher, senior partner at Midwest Family Broadcasting, was the last person I interviewed for this book. I asked him what he thought his legacy would be.

"God, I don't know," was his initial response.

On further reflection, he said, "The best thing about being a sales manager is setting goals and accomplishing your goals. Setting personal goals and setting corporate goals and getting people on the same page with you. And providing the leadership."

The day after the interview, Phil called me back. "I've been going through some old files of mine and I thought you might like to see some of the letters people have written me over the years. He had kept letters from customers, salespeople, and his company's management team.

The letters were truly touching and personal, and it was obvious as I read them over why he saved and cherished them.

Here's my favorite letter:

Just a note from one of the former WISM good guys. Phil, you're probably wondering why I'm writing. Well, it's just a little bit of nostalgia.

The other day I started thinking over my career and realized the years I spent at WISM were among the best. Truly, it was a memorable time.

Further, I want you to know, at this late date, that you were a great boss. A bit of an SOB at times, but very fair and a good leader. I learned a great deal from you. In fact, I still find myself applying concepts I learned at your knee.

Phil, I hope your health is good, hope your life is good.
Sincerely,
Glenn

On that note, I can only hope that you learned lessons in this book that will give you the tools to develop and discipline your sales team so that one day you might get a letter or two like that one.

INDEX